INSIGHT COMPACT GUIDES

JERUSALEM

Compact Guide: Jerusalem is the ideal quick-reference guide to the Holy City. It tells you all you need to know about Jerusalem's attractions, from the Arab Bazaar to the Western Wall and the Dome of the Rock to the Mount of Olives, as well as guiding you to some classic destinations outside the city.

This is one of nearly 100 titles in *Apa Publications'* top-value series of pocket-sized, easy-to-use guidebooks intended for the independent-minded traveller. *Compact Guides* are in essence travel encyclopedias in miniature, designed to be comprehensive yet portable, as well as up-to-date and authoritative.

Star Attractions

An instant reference to some of Jerusalem's top attractions to help you set your priorities.

Western Wall p18

Dome of the Rock p19

Church of the Holy Sepulchre p24

Me'a She'arim p32

Makhane Yehuda Market p41

Shrine of the Book p42

Ein Kerem p49

Bethlehem p51

Jericho p55

Kumran p56

Jaffa p59

JERUSALEM

Jerusalem — The Holy City

Opposite: Jerusalem from the Mount of Olives

Jerusalem excites religious passions among pilgrims, but more surprisingly the Holy City has the ability to captivate non-religious visitors too. For above and beyond the fascinating religious history and archaeology, Jerusalem's breathtaking mountain views, graceful gardens and elegant architecture can stir the soul of the most cynical atheist. Spirituality aside, Jerusalem is also a sensual, romantic city, perhaps lacking the verve and vigour of nearby Tel Aviv but nevertheless having a vibrant nightlife with the restaurant and pub district crowded well into the early hours of the morning.

However, Jerusalem is first and foremost the cradle of monotheism – sacred to Jew, Christian and Muslim. It was here that King David established the capital of the ancient Israelites 3,000 years ago and his son King Solomon built the resplendent Temple. It was here that Christ, according to tradition, was sentenced to death, crucified, buried and rose from the dead. And it was from here Muslims believe that the prophet Mohammed ascended to heaven.

Church of All Nations
Jewish scholar

All these beliefs have led to conflict. The Christians today have no political claims on the city, though the holy sites are jealously looked after and dozens of different churches own much of Jerusalem. Today it is Jew and Muslim who dispute the city, although the modern conflict is more nationalistic than religious. Jerusalem is the capital of modern Israel, while Arab East Jerusalem is claimed by the PLO as the capital of Palestine. The Israelis themselves are deeply divided between secular and ultra-orthodox Jews.

5

Despite these tensions, visitors will be surprised by the sense of daily social harmony which prevails. Occasional terrorist outrages capture media headlines but with little criminal violence, Jerusalem is safer than most European and American cities.

Strategic location

Ancient maps often portray Jerusalem as the centre of the world. This is not entirely a religiously zealous interpretation, for before the discovery of America, Jerusalem and the entire Holy Land's position at the crossroads of the three known continents – Asia, Africa and Europe did give it a global centrality.

Jerusalem lies at 35°20' longitude and 31°80' latitude. To the west lies the Mediterranean coastal plain and the most populated region of Israel. The sea itself is some 48km (30 miles) west of Jerusalem. To the north, east and south of the city is the West Bank, captured by Israel from Jordan

Desert at Masada and blooms in Liberty Bell Park

Maintaining security

in 1967, though most of the cities have been given to the Palestinian Authority. The rest of the area, Samaria to the north and Judea to the south, remains a subject of dispute between Israel and the Palestinians.

Some 40km (25 miles) east of Jerusalem is the border with Jordan near the Palestinian autonomous zone of Jericho. The River Jordan flows through the Syrian African Rift Valley and into the Dead Sea, which at 400 metres (1,300ft) below sea level is the lowest point on earth.

Mountain climate

Jerusalem itself is on a mountain peak over 800 metres (2,550ft) above sea level. This altitude means that the city has a cool climate despite its southerly latitude. Though summer temperatures usually top 30°C (86°F), evening breezes often make a sweater mandatory even in August. And unlike the coastal plain which is uncomfortably humid, the inland hills are dry. Spring and autumn provide the most pleasant weather, while winter in Jerusalem can be cold with heavy rains between November and March and even rare flurries of light snow. But though the thermometer can dip to zero there are also long spells of bright winter sunshine when temperatures reach 20°C (68°F).

Jerusalem is one of the lowest peaks in the Judean Mountains. Ramallah to the north and Hebron to the south are both 900 metres (3,000ft) high and it was probably this, combined with a series of easily negotiated valleys to the west and east, that made Jerusalem a strategic crossroads in ancient times. Another factor persuading the Jebusites to settle here was an underground spring.

Disputed capital

Since King David established Jerusalem as the Israelite capital, Jews have viewed Jerusalem as their holiest city. Throughout the Diaspora they have always faced Jerusalem when praying. So it was only natural that Jerusalem was declared the capital of the modern State of Israel shortly after its establishment in 1948. The Knesset, Israel's parliament, elected at least every four years by proportional representation, is in Jerusalem. The Prime Minister, chosen every four years by the electorate, has his office in Jerusalem. The Supreme Court, most government offices and the Bank of Israel are in the capital. The President, a titular head of state chosen every five years, has his residence in Jerusalem.

Yet almost all foreign embassies are located in Tel Aviv. Under the UN partition plan of 1948, Jerusalem was meant to be an international city ruled by the UN, but following the War of Independence Israel occupied the western half of the city and Jordan the eastern part. Israel proceeded to annexe East Jerusalem after the Six Day War in 1967. While Israeli sovereignty over the western part of the city has been fully recognised by the world, the question of who rules East Jerusalem remains at the heart of the Israel-Palestinian conflict. The Palestinians claim East Jerusalem as their capital and New Orient House and various other offices act as national Palestinian institutions.

But even Israelis do not behave as if Jerusalem is fully the country's capital. If Jerusalem is the political capital, then Tel Aviv is the country's economic and cultural centre. The country's banks, industrial conglomerates, newspapers and even some government offices are headquartered in Tel Aviv. Jerusalem is seen by Tel Aviv's secular population as a city of Arabs and ultra-orthodox Jews.

Jaffa alleyway

A colourful mosaic

To be sure, the majority of Jerusalem's 600,000 residents are either Arab (30 percent) or ultra-orthodox Jews (25 percent). Nevertheless, the reins of power are held firmly by the secular and modern orthodox Jews who comprise about 45 percent of the city's population. Both the current mayor, Ehud Olmert, from the right-wing Likud, and his left-wing predecessor, Teddy Kollek, who ruled the city from 1965 to 1993, are staunchly secular figures who built successful coalitions with the ultra-orthodox Jewish political parties. The city's Arabs, who have had the right to vote since Jerusalem was annexed by Israel in 1967, have consistently refused to do so, claiming that they are Palestinian rather than Israeli citizens.

Arab shopper

But it would be over-simplistic to speak of the city's population solely in terms of its religious groupings. Teddy Kollek referred to the city as a delicate mosaic with each community knowing its place, shape and colour in the scheme of things and eager to perpetuate its traditions.

Of the city's 200,000 non-Jews, some 85 percent are Muslims. This is a relatively homogeneous population showing allegiance to the Palestinian national movement but ranging from Muslim fundamentalists through to secular but very conservative family-oriented Arabs. Though heavily politicised, Jerusalem's Palestinians take a more pragmatic approach towards co-existence with Israel. Unlike their cousins in Gaza and the West Bank, the city's Arabs come into daily contact with Jews who are not soldiers and therefore tend to demonize them less. Much of the wealthy middle class is dependent on tourism, which clearly suffers when political tensions escalate.

An ecumenical nightmare

The city's 30,000 indigenous Christians also identify with the Palestinian national movement but will privately say they are of Greek or Armenian rather than Arab origin. The Greek Orthodox church, with a community of more

A hallowed site

Russian Orthodox women

The Druze have their own religion

than 20,000 has the largest number of adherents. There are 2,000 Armenians living in Jerusalem's Old City and nearly 6,000 Catholics, not only Latins but autonomous sects such as the Greek Catholics, Armenian Catholics and Maronites. Inter-marriage among the Christian sects and with middle-class Muslims is not uncommon.

In addition to the indigenous Christian community there are tens of thousands of other Christians residing in Jerusalem, usually attached to the various churches, monasteries and seminaries around the city, as well as thousands of long-stay believers drawn to the Holy City.

Perhaps the biggest surprise for visiting Christians from the west is the vast number of sects. Generally speaking, the newer the church the less conspicuous its presence. The Armenian Orthodox, Ethiopian Orthodox and Russian Orthodox churches possess major properties throughout the city. The Greek Orthodox and Catholics own large swathes of the city. And lesser known churches such as the Copts, Syrian Orthodox, Chaldean Orthodox, Georgian Orthodox and Southern Indian churches have a significant presence. In contrast, the Protestant churches have only a few institutions. Yet ecumenical harmony and respect prevails because the churches have little to fight over locally, save theology. The exception is over ownership of various parts of the Church of the Holy Sepulchre which has caused violent confrontations down the centuries.

Degrees of orthodoxy

Though Jerusalem has a far higher percentage of religious Jews than elsewhere in Israel, most of the city's Jews are secular and share the liberal, humanistic outlook of their Western European and North American counterparts. These secular Jews hold power but feel besieged by both the black-hatted ultra-orthodox Jews and Arabs, both of whom have a far higher birth rate. Moreover, they are less faithful to Jerusalem and leave the city in larger numbers for a better job or livelier singles scene.

Secular Jews are divided by their ethnic origins and comprise an Ashkenazi (European) minority and Sephardi (Oriental) majority. The Ashkenazim are more middle-class and left-wing while the Sephardim are more working class, traditional and right-wing but inter-marriage is common. A secular Jew has more in common with a Palestinian than a black-hatted ultra-orthodox Jew but there is little social intercourse because of the Israel-Arab conflict. Israeli and Palestinian neighbourhoods are strictly segregated – through mutual consent, not legislation.

Between secular Jewry and ultra-orthodox Jewry are some 100,000 modern orthodox Jews who have more in common with secular Jewry but sympathise with many values of the black-hatted Jews.

It's good to talk

Me'a She'arim, to the northeast of the city centre, is the spiritual heart of ultra-orthodox Jewry, whose adherents reject every aspect and value of modern living. The ultra-orthodox way of life has more to do with medieval Poland and Russia than the biblical Middle East, as the dress code indicates. The Sabbath dress includes fur hats that seem out of place in the blistering Levantine heat. The women usually stay at home tending to their large broods. The ultra-orthodox are by no means as uniform as they seem and include many sects, most of them headquartered in New York, ranging from the Satmar, who vehemently oppose the existence of Israel because the messiah has not yet come, through to the Lubavitcher, who fiercely oppose giving up any land to the Arabs but tend not to serve in the army because praying is considered a more effective way of vanquishing the enemy than fighting.

9

Between desert and forest

Every bit as diverse as the city's residents is the flora and fauna around Jerusalem. To the west are forests, while to the east is desert. The forests, mainly pine, are especially attractive in the late winter and early spring, after the heavy rains and before the searing sun parches the countryside. First the hillsides are ablaze with the pink and white hues of almond blossom and then wild flowers – red anemones, pink cyclamen and blue orchids. Other treats include fleeting glimpses of gazelles and the occasional tortoise. The terraced hillsides with olive groves and grapevines have a distinctly biblical feel. However, visitors from northern climes will be more impressed by the stunning landscapes and canyons of the Judean Desert to the east. Wildlife is sparse here, but keep an eye open for the ibex, a majestic-looking mountain goat, and the hyrax, a rabbit-like creature which is a relative of the elephant.

Springtime in the Holy Land

Historical Highlights

c8000BC Some of the world's first agricultural settlements are established in the region.

c3000BC As city kingdoms develop based on trade between Egypt and Mesopotamia, the area around Jerusalem is settled by the Jebusites, a Canaanite tribe.

c2000BC According to Genesis, Abraham travels to a distant hilltop as commanded by God in order to sacrifice his son. Orthodox Jews and Muslims believe that the mountain peak was Mount Moriah on which the Temple was to be built over 1,000 years later.

c1000BC King David decides to establish a new capital on land not associated with a particular tribe to help unite the Children of Israel. He defeats the Jebusites and moves his capital from Hebron to Jerusalem. The site of David's city, with access to an underground spring, is outside of the Old City of today, just south of the Dung Gate.

c950BC King Solomon builds the First Temple to house the Ark of the Covenant and consolidates Jerusalem's position as the Israelite capital.

925BC After Solomon's death his kingdom is split and Jerusalem becomes the capital of Judah.

586BC Nebuchadnezzar, the Babylonian ruler, captures Jerusalem, destroys the Temple and takes the Jews into exile.The Babylonians are subsequently defeated by the Persians who allow the Jews to return to Jerusalem.

520BC The Second Temple is built.

333BC Alexander the Great conquers Jerusalem. After his death in 323BC, subsequent Greek rulers restrict Jewish worship.

301BC The Egyptian Greeks led by Ptolemy I capture Jerusalem.

198BC The Damascus based Seleucid Greeks seize control of Jerusalem. After the Seleucids defile the Temple in 164BC, the Hasmonean brothers successfully lead an uprising restoring Jewish sovereignty to Jerusalem. The Temple is re-consecrated.

63BC The Romans conquer Jerusalem after a dispute between two Hasmonean rivals.

37BC King Herod I ascends the throne and begins a reign of terror, but also accomplishes many grandiose projects including major additions to the Second Temple.

6AD After King Herod II's death, Jerusalem comes under the direct rule of Roman procurators. One of them is a man called Pontius Pilate.

30AD During a period of popular unrest, a Galilee preacher, Jesus Christ, is crucified by the Romans.

66 The Jewish insurrection against Rome begins. Four years later, the Romans recapture Jerusalem and destroy the Temple, leaving only a part of the Western Wall standing.

130 Emperor Hadrian destroys parts of Jerusalem in preparation for the construction of a new Roman colony. This sparks off the failed Bar Kochba revolt which results in the exile of the Jews. Six years later, Jerusalem is renamed Aeolina Capitolina by the Romans and becomes a completely non-Jewish city.

325 Constantine the Great converts the entire Eastern Roman Empire to Christianity and the following year he sends his mother Queen Helena to Jerusalem from Byzantium (Constantinople) to identify the holy sites. The sacred locations chosen by Helena in Jerusalem such as the Via Dolorosa and the Church of the Holy Sepulchre are still believed by the Orthodox and Catholic churches to be the site of Christ's crucifixion, burial and resurrection.

361 Julian the Apostate allows Jews to resettle in Jerusalem.

614 The Persians conquer Jerusalem, but 15 years later Heraclius retakes the city.

638 The Muslim conquest of Jerusalem.

691 The Dome of the Rock is built on the Temple Mount on the site where Muslims believe that Mohammed ascended to heaven. The construction of the El-Aksa Mosque follows in 705.

750 Abassid caliphs succeed the Umayyads.

969 Fatimid caliphs take control; in 1009 caliph Al-Hakim destroys the Church of the Holy Sepulchre and other Christian shrines.

1071 The Turkish Seljuks conquer the city.

1099 Crusaders massacre most of the population and establish the Kingdom of Jerusalem. Church of the Holy Sepulchre consecrated in 1149.

1187 Saladin defeats the Crusaders and conquers Jerusalem.

1260 Mamelukes, Asian warriors who had seized power in Egypt, conquer the entire Holy Land. Jerusalem begins centuries of decline.

1516 Ottoman Turks capture Jerusalem. In 1541, Suleiman the Magnificent completes construction of Jerusalem's walls.

1832 Egyptian ruler Muhammed Ali captures Jerusalem but the Ottomans retake the city after eight years.

1840 The world's imperial powers open consulates in Jerusalem and begin building religious institutions, vying for influence in the Holy Land.

1860 The first Jewish and Christian settlements are set up outside the city walls.

1898 Kaiser Wilhelm II of Germany visits Jerusalem and meets, among others, Theodore Herzl, the founder of modern political Zionism.

1917 The British capture Jerusalem. The Ottomans surrender without a shot being fired. British Foreign Secretary Lord Balfour declares support for a Jewish homeland in Palestine. Three years later, Arab riots in Jerusalem and elsewhere make the British rethink the Balfour Declaration.

1925 The Hebrew University opens on Mount Scopus as Jewish immigration rises sharply.

1929 Intensified Arab riots and Jewish reprisals; ethnic violence escalates throughout the 1930s.

1933 Adolf Hitler assumes power in Germany but Jewish immigration is subsequently curtailed by British restrictions.

1946 After the horrors of the Holocaust become known, right-wing Jewish activists become more militant and blow up British Army HQ in Jerusalem's King David Hotel.

1947 UN General Assembly calls for the partition of Palestine with Jerusalem to become an international UN administered city.

1948 The State of Israel is declared. The War of Independence breaks out as five Arab armies invade Israel. The Jordanians capture the eastern part of the city including all the holy sites, while the Israeli army takes the western part of the city.

1949 Israel declares Jerusalem its capital, and the Knesset parliament is moved from Tel Aviv.

1950 Jordan officially annexes East Jerusalem and the West Bank.

1965 The Israel Museum opens its doors. Exhibits include the Dead Sea Scrolls.

1967 The city's division comes to an end during the Six Day War as Israel captures the eastern part of the city from Jordan and then annexes it.

1978 Egyptian President Anwar Sadat visits Jerusalem and an Israel-Egypt peace accord is signed the following year.

1987 The Intifada ends 20 years of relatively peaceful co-existence between the city's Jews and Arabs, though the intensity of the violence is much less than in the West Bank and Gaza.

1993 The Intifada ends following the peace agreement between Israel and the PLO.

1994 Israel signs a peace accord with Jordan which talks of the Hashemite Kingdom's special responsibilities for the Muslim Holy Sites.

1995 Prime Minister Yitzhak Rabin is assassinated at a Tel Aviv peace rally.

1996 Riots break out over the opening of the Hasmonean Tunnel linking the Western Wall with the Via Dolorosa.

1997 The peace process becomes deadlocked after Israel begins construction of a new neighbourhood in the southern suburb of Har Homa.

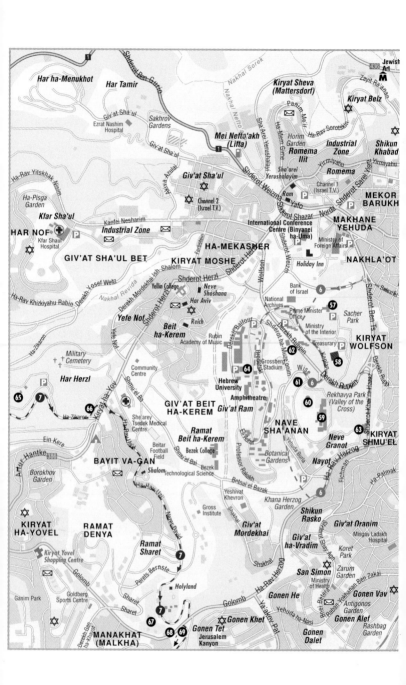

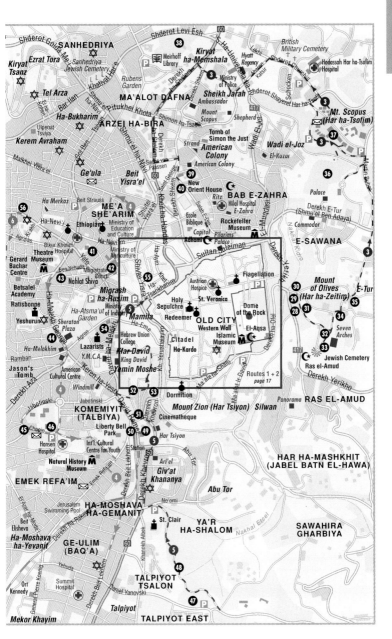

15

6

Reliable charges

Preceding pages:
Damascus Gate

David's Tower

Route 1

The Old City

The Arab Market – The Jewish Quarter – The Western Wall – The Temple Mount – City of David – Mount Zion *See map on page 17*

This route begins at the Jaffa Gate and focuses on the southern half of the Old City, taking in the souvenir shop section of the Arab market and the sites holy to Jews and Muslims. Remember to dress modestly, keeping arms and legs covered. After a foray outside of the city walls to David's City and Mount Zion, this circular walk returns to the Jaffa Gate via the Armenian Quarter. The entire Old City covers one square kilometre (half a square mile) and the impressive walls were built in the 16th century by the Ottoman ruler Suleiman the Magnificent.

Jaffa Gate (Sha'ar Yafo), where this tour begins and ends, is the only gate into the Old City where the wall has been breached in order to make a road. This was done in 1898 so that Kaiser Wilhelm II of Germany and his entourage could enter the Old City on horseback when he made a pilgrimage to Jerusalem. The Jaffa Gate, facing west to Jaffa and south to Bethlehem and Hebron, has historically been one of the Old City's principal thoroughfares. In Arabic it is called Bab el-Khalil – the Hebron Gate. On the left just inside the gate is a tourist information office, while 75 metres up on the right, at the beginning of Armenian Patriarchate Street, is the Christian Information Centre.

To the right of the gate is ★★ **David's Tower** ❶ and the **Citadel Museum of the History of Jerusalem** ❶ (Sunday to Friday 10am–4pm, Saturday 10am–2pm), which can be entered from opposite the Christian Information Centre. Built on the site of a Herodian palace, David's Tower has nothing to do with David and served as the city's main fortress for over 2,000 years. Archaeological excavations reveal the history of the site. The oldest remains are of a defensive tower built by the Hasmoneans in the 2nd century BC, and there is also the base of a huge tower built by Herod to protect his palace. The ramparts were built by the Mamelukes in the 14th century, and the top of the tower offers a splendid view of the Old City. The interior halls contain a state-of-the-art exhibition attractively depicting the history of Jerusalem, and the complex also contains a 19th-century model of the Old City, crafted in zinc by a Hungarian, Stephen Illes, in 1872.

Enter the ★★ **Arab bazaar** ❷ via David Street (El-Bazar), a continuation of the road leading in from the Jaffa Gate. The exotic hustle and bustle in the narrow alleyways of the market combined with the rich smells of leather, coffee and spices can either be exhilarating or claustrophobic. Aggressive store owners will hustle passers by. There is no need to be in any hurry to buy. All the shops sell similar items and vendors will ask ridiculously high prices, expecting to be bargained down.

In the bowels of the bazaar

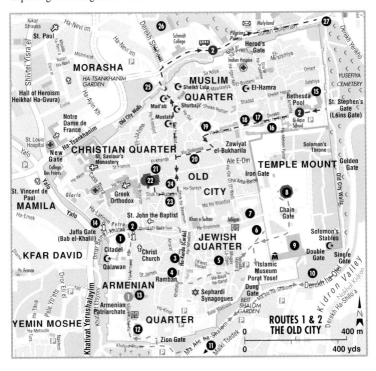

Deep in the bowels of the bazaar, just before the T-junction at the end of David Street, is a right turn into ★ **Ha-Kardo ❸**, the main north-south city street during Byzantine times. It has been pleasantly restored and contains a collection of upmarket souvenir shops. After 40 metres there is an archway marking the border between the Muslim and Jewish Quarters.

At the end of the Kardo there is a staircase on the left leading up to Beit El Street opposite. On the left is the entrance to a large square, before which is a huge stone arch. This is all that remains of the **Hurva ❹**, which was the Old City's largest synagogue until it was razed to the ground along with the entire Jewish Quarter by the Jordanians following the War of Independence in 1948.

Across the square is Tiferet Yisrael which leads eastwards. On the left is the ★ **Burnt House ❺** (Sunday to Thursday 9am–5pm, Friday 9am–1pm). Discovered in 1970, the Burnt House was owned in Roman times by the priestly Kathros family. Artefacts found within include pottery vessels, a ceramic inkwell, mortars, pestles and weights. A spear and severed human arm found on the site suggest that the family met a violent end when the Romans captured Jerusalem after their siege in 70AD, and the house's charred remains indicate that it was burned down.

Opposite the end of Tiferet Yisrael is a staircase called Ma'alot Rabi Yehuda Halevi leading down to the ★★★ **Western Wall ❻**. The Western Wall, also known as the Wailing Wall, is the only remaining structure from the Temple, which was destroyed by the Romans in 70AD. Comprising large stone blocks, this modest wall, which was and still is a retaining wall for the Temple Mount complex, is considered the holiest shrine in Judaism. Men and women must enter separate parts of the wall – men

Burnt House exhibits

Observances at the Western Wall

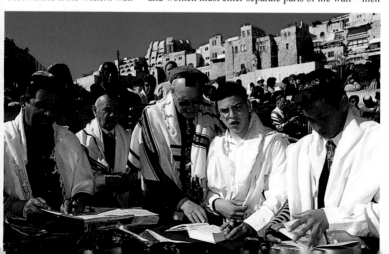

to the left and women to the right (men must cover their head with a 'kippa' which is provided at the entrance). Jewish custom is to place 'prayer notes' into the wall in the hope that personal requests will receive a divine response. The cynical have therefore nicknamed the wall 'God's Post Office', and it is even possible to send faxes to a telecommunications company representative, who will place the message in the wall (02-5612222).

Hasmonean Tunnel

In front of the entrance to the wall on the left is the ★ **Hasmonean Tunnel** ❼ (advance booking only, tel: 02-6271333). The tunnel, which was a principal thoroughfare during Hasmonean times and runs beneath the western perimeter of the Temple Mount, was opened in 1987, but there were violent Arab protests when a second entrance was opened on to the Via Dolorosa in 1996.

To the right of the Western Wall a path leads up to the **Temple Mount**, known in Hebrew as *Har ha-Bayit* and in Arabic as *Haram Esh Sharif*. The area beyond the Maghariba Gate, one of 10 gates leading into the Temple Mount, is controlled by the Muslim Wakf religious trust and non-Muslims are not allowed to visit after midday and on Fridays. Officially, orthodox Jews are not allowed to visit the Temple Mount because of the fear that they will violate the Holy of Holies, the part of the Temple where according to tradition the High Priest would converse with God, and where all other Jews were forbidden to enter. But some nationalist Jews claim that it is known that the Holy of Holies was in the northern part of the Temple complex and that this prohibition is simply a political ploy to keep Jews and Arabs apart on this most sensitive piece of real estate.

On the ascent to Temple Mount

The Temple Mount, which comprises nearly 20 percent of the Old City, surprises most visitors with its vastness, demonstrating how large the Temple itself must have been. The area is dominated by the magnificent ★★★ **Dome of the Rock** ❽ in the northern part of the Temple Mount and the ★★ **El Aqsa Mosque** ❾ to the south. Tickets to enter these two buildings are on sale from a kiosk in front of the El Aqsa Mosque and shoes must be removed before entering each of them.

The Dome of the Rock

The Dome of the Rock is an impressive edifice. The exterior is decorated in an exquisite mosaic of painted tiles, marble and stained glass in delicate hues of blue, green and gold with Koranic inscriptions. The domed roof was recently covered in 25-carat gold. Built in 691 by the Caliph Abd al-Malik, who was horrified by the neglect of the Temple Mount, the building was refurbished in the 16th century by Suleiman the Magnificent in the highly aesthetic decorative style that we see today. The interior is no less ornate. Dozens of Persian rugs carpet the floor

1❾

Dome decoration

while the domed roof contains a mosaic with complex and colourful motifs.

The Dome of the Rock is a shrine rather than a mosque and the focal point of the octagonal building is the **Foundation Stone** in the centre. Muslims and Jews believe that the world was created here, and that Abraham came here to Mount Moriah to sacrifice his son, as related in Genesis. Muslims believe that Mohammed ascended to heaven from here on his horse after his death in Medina.

The silver-domed El Aqsa Mosque was built in 705. The Crusaders converted it into a palace for the Templars but it became a mosque again after being captured by Saladin in 1187. In 1951, King Abdullah of Jordan (King Hussein's grandfather) was assassinated here while praying, and in 1969 an Australian Christian fanatic burned much of the interior. While the exterior is unremarkable compared to the Dome of the Rock, the interior contains lavish Persian rugs and richly embellished decorations.

Other sites of interest on the Temple Mount include **Solomon's Stables** in the southeastern corner. This cavernous hall, which was used as a stables by the Crusaders, was recently converted into a mosque, and is closed to non-Muslims. The **Islamic Museum**, to the west of El Aqsa Mosque, displays artifacts depicting Islamic life in Jerusalem. Entry to the museum is included in the price of the ticket for the Dome of the Rock and the El Aqsa Mosque.

Islamic Museum exhibit

The City of David

Back down from the Maghariba Gate, on the left are excavations from the ★ **City of David** ❿. Part of these excavations outside of the Old City, which can be reached by turning left at the other side of the Dung Gate, have been made into an archaeological park (Ha-Ofel). Indeed most of the original city established by King David was outside of the Old City walls and it was King Solomon who brought the city onto the higher ground by building the Temple. The remains are unremarkable save for Warren's Shaft, named after the 19th-century British archaeologist who identified it, which peers down to the tunnel built by Hezekiah in 700BC to link the Gihon Spring, from which ancient Jerusalem drew its water supply, to a pool beneath the Old City. It is also possible to wade knee-deep through Hezekiah's Tunnel which can be reached via steps leading down opposite the archaeological garden.

Further along the road towards the Mount of Olives is a recently completed promenade which looks out over the Jewish cemetery opposite and the Kidron Valley. Jews believe that when the Messiah comes, those buried on the Mount of Olives will be the first to return to life. Beneath the mount is the **Tomb of Absalom**, a huge cylindrical mausoleum carved out of the mountainside, where tradition has it that King David's son Absalom is buried. The Kidron Valley was historically one of the major routes eastwards down to the Dead Sea.

Backtracking up the hill for about 600 metres is ★ **Mount Zion** ⓫ (Har Tsiyon). Legend has it that Suleiman the Magnificent beheaded the builder of the city walls for forgetting to place Mount Zion inside the Old City. Mount Zion looks down into the Hinnom Valley and gazing down on this pleasant pastoral scene it is difficult to comprehend that the location was historically associated with hell. A leper's colony probably existed in the valley.

The most conspicuous building on Mount Zion is the **Church of the Dormition**, a German Catholic institution built in 1910, on the site where according to tradition the Virgin Mary died. To the left of the church is a two-storey building containing **King David's Tomb**, on the ground floor (Sunday to Thursday 8am–5pm, Friday 8am–1pm), though historians doubt that this is David's real burial chamber. On the first floor of the building through a separate entrance is the **Coenaculum** (daily 8.30am–5pm), the supposed site of Christ's Last Supper. The belief is that the Last Supper took place adjacent to David's tomb, so those sceptical about the burial of the king here will also doubt the Coenaculum.

Re-entering the Old City through the nearby **Zion Gate** the entrance to the ★ **Armenian Quarter** can be reached by turning left. The **Armenian Museum** ⓬ (Monday to Saturday 10am–5pm), just along on the right, exhibits paintings, frescoes, books and other items reflecting the history of the Armenian people and documents its genocide by the Turks during World War I. There is also an exhibition of exquisite Armenian stone floors and ceramic tiles, and a display about the Armenian alphabet and its supposed divine origins. But the real highlight is a collection of 3,000 manuscripts dating from the 9th century, many of them with detailed and delightful illustrations.

The Armenian Quarter itself (weekdays from 3–3.30pm and on Saturday and Sunday from 2.30–3.15pm) is a walled city within a walled city and it was set up by Armenian pilgrims 1,000 years ago. The entrance is further along towards the Jaffa Gate. The focal point is the **Church of St James** ⓭ built in the 12th century over the ruins of a 7th-century Byzantine chapel.

Back along the road at the Jaffa Gate, and indeed at any of the city's seven gates, it is possible to climb onto the ★ **Rampart Walk** ⓮ (Sunday to Thursday 9am–5pm, Friday 9am–3pm). This secure path on top of the Old City walls offers marvellous views.

Mount Zion: Church of the Dormition

King David's Tomb and the Coenaculum

Route 2

The Old City

The Via Dolorosa – The Church of the Holy Sepulchre – The Arab Market – The Garden Tomb – Rockefeller Museum *See map on page 17*

Pilgrim in procession

This walk begins at St Stephen's Gate and encompasses the northern half of the Old City and includes the sites most sacred to Christianity. The visitor can journey along the 14 Stations of the Cross in the Via Dolorosa and Church of the Holy Sepulchre which Orthodox and Catholic Christians believe was the very route Christ took before his crucifixion. Protestants are more circumspect and many suggest that the site of Christ's burial was in the Garden Tomb which lays outside of the Old City walls near the Damascus Gate. The Holy Sepulchre was identified in the 4th century by Queen Helena, Emperor Constantine's mother, while the Stations of the Cross along the Via Dolorosa only became institutionalised several centuries ago. Britain's General Gordon identified the Garden Tomb. In any event, dress modestly when visiting all these sites.

St Stephen's Gate

St Stephen's Gate takes its English name from the belief that St Stephen was martyred near here. But in Hebrew and Arabic this is called the Lion's Gate because of the two pairs of lions carved in relief just outside the gate. Legend has it that the Ottoman ruler Suleiman the Magnificent had a dream in which he was mauled by four lions. His advisors interpreted the dream as an expression of God's anger because the Holy City lay neglected with its walls destroyed. Suleiman thus undertook to rebuild the walls. It was via the steep, narrow lane leading up to St Stephen's Gate that Israeli troops first entered the Old City in 1967 during the Six Day War.

The gate is also referred to as Our Lady Mary's Gate because just inside on the right is ★ **The Church of St Anne ⑮**. Belonging to the White Fathers, a French Roman Catholic order, this Crusader-built church and monastery stands on the site which has traditionally been thought of as the birthplace of the Virgin Mary and the home of her parents Joachim and Anne. A rock hewn crypt beneath the church is the supposed site of Mary's birth. The complex also includes the **Pool of Betheseda** where Christ is believed to have tended the sick and endowed the water with curative powers. Opposite the church is the Gate of the Tribes leading to the Temple Mount.

About 200 metres along the lane there is a small path leading up to the **Omariya Boys School ⑯**. Tradition has it that this is the site where Christ was sentenced to death by Pilate. This is the **First Station** along the ★★ **Via Dolorosa** but access into the school, which also commands an excellent view of the Temple Mount, is not always possible. Every Friday at 3pm, the Franciscans lead a procession down the Via Dolorosa from here. A little further on is the **Second Station** within the **Church of the Flagellation** ⓱. Despite its medieval style, this church was only built in the 1920s and it stands on the spot where Christ was beaten by the Romans and had a crown of thorns placed on his head. The church stands within a Franciscan complex (daily 8am–noon and 2pm–5pm) which is opposite the northern exit of the Hasmonean Tunnel. The complex also includes the **Franciscan Biblical School** which has an exhibition of archeological finds and the **Church of the Condemnation**, built in 1910, where Christ was given his cross.

Further along the Via Dolorosa is the **Convent of the Sisters of Zion** ⓲, distinguished by the **Ecce Homo Arch**, a 2nd-century edifice, which crosses the alleyway. Here, too, is an archaeological collection, but of most interest is the **Lithostrotos** (daily 8.30am–12.30pm and 2–4pm) beneath the convent, where the original Roman paving stones, that Christ may have trodden on with the cross, can be seen. There are also underground pools which were part of the city's complex water system.

Several hundred metres down the lane and the Via Dolorosa turns left at the junction into Ha-Gai (El Wad) street. On the right at the turn is the **Austrian Hospice** ⓳, a mid-19th century building that was recently converted from a hospital back into a hospice offering a very comfortable old-world Middle European charm for its guests. On the left along Ha-Gai, just after the Armenian Patriarchate, the **Third Station**, where Christ fell under the weight of the cross, is marked on the wall.

Via Dolorosa: the Lithostrotos and the Second Station

The Fourth Station

At the Seventh Station

Church of the Holy Sepulchre

Almost immediately afterwards is the **Fourth Station** where Christ encountered his mother. In the crypt of the **Armenian Catholic Church of Our Lady of the Spasm** is a Byzantine mosaic depicting the outline of Mary's sandals where she supposedly stood as her son passed.

The Via Dolorosa turns right and on the first house on the left at the junction is the **Fifth Station** where Christ is believed to have leaned against the wall, overburdened by the weight of the cross. A Franciscan chapel built here in 1895 is named for Simon of Cyrene, whom the Romans forced at this point to help Christ carry the cross. Further up the alleyway on the right is the store of the **Karakashian** family whose stylish Armenian pottery offers a tasteful souvenir of the city.

The Sixth Station on the left near the pottery store is by the **Greek Catholic Church of Veronica ⑳**. According to tradition it was here that St Veronica wiped Christ's brow with her veil. **The Seventh Station** is found at the corner of the Via Dolorosa and Beit ha-Bad Street (Suk Khan-E-Zeit Street) and it was here that Christ fell for the second time. A chapel belonging to the Copts stands on the site, which is also called the Gate of Judgement, believed to be one of the city gates in Roman times.

At this point the Via Dolorosa runs to the left along the alley of the main Arab market. **The Eighth Station** is on the opposite corner of the junction just up El Khanqa Street outside the **Greek Orthodox Chapel of St Chrlampos** and it was here that Christ supposedly said 'Do not weep for me, weep for Jerusalem.'

The Ninth Station, where Christ fell for the third and final time, is located in the doorway of the ★★ **Coptic Patriarchate Compound ㉑** which is along Beit ha-Bad Street and up a wide staircase to the right. Resembling an African village, this delightful compound has been a roof-top Ethiopian Orthodox monastery since the 17th century. The roof is that of the Church of the Holy Sepulchre, and it is the subject of a bitter ownership dispute between the Coptic and Ethiopian Orthodox churches. It is possible to enter the Holy Sepulchre from the compound but preferable, and less confusing, to enter via the front entrance, which can be reached by returning to Beit ha-Bad Street and journeying right and right again into Shuk ha-Tsabaim (Suk Ed Dabbagha).

★★★ **The Church of the Holy Sepulchre ㉒** is reached via a small doorway leading into a large plaza at the end of Shuk ha-Tsabaim. The last five stations are located inside the church, which was built in 1149 by the Crusaders on the site of a Byzantine chapel which had been destroyed first by the Persians in the 7th century and then by Caliph Al-Hakim in the 11th century. The various parts of this confusing building, crammed with

At the altar

icons, mosaics, frescoes, paintings and other decorations are owned by the Catholics, Greek Orthodox, Ethiopian Orthodox, Armenian Orthodox and Coptic churches, who are always feuding over ownership rights. As a result, the keys to the front door (the church is opened daily from dawn to dusk) are held by a Muslim family and repairs are undertaken by the Israeli government.

25

To the right of the entrance is a steep stairway leading up to Calvary, the rock on which Christ was believed to have been crucified. On the right is a Franciscan chapel containing the **10th and 11th Stations** where Christ was stripped and nailed to the cross. In the adjoining Greek Orthodox chapel on the left is the **12th Station** where Christ was allegedly crucified, while back in the Franciscan chapel is the **13th Station** where Christ's body was handed over to Mary. Back downstairs is the **14th Station**. This can only be reached by almost crawling into a small rotunda where the tomb of Christ is found beneath a raised marble slab.

Crusader crosses in the church

After leaving the church and returning to Shuk ha-Tsabaim (Suk Ed Dabbagha), those with Protestant sensibilities may wish to meditate for a while in the **Church of the Redeemer** ㉓, situated about 30 metres to the right of the entrance to the Holy Sepulchre's plaza. This German Lutheran church, the tallest edifice in the Old City, was completed about 100 years ago. The austere and silent atmosphere inside, in contrast to the hustle and bustle of the Holy Sepulchre, will appeal to the more puritanical.

A little along from the Church of the Redeemer is the Russian Orthodox **Alexander Nevski Church** ㉔. This pink stone building, erected in 1887, has some fascinating archaeological remains in its basement, including parts of the original Roman road and an entrance into the original Byzantine chapel of the Sepulchre.

Damascus Gate by night

The Garden Tomb

Back now in the direction of the Damascus Gate and into the heart of the Arab market. This is where the locals go shopping for food and clothes, and this is the place to buy coffee, spices, inexpensive olive oil or other local delicacies like *bakhlawa* – sticky, sweet cakes.

★ **Damascus Gate** is the principal thoroughfare between the Old City and Arab East Jerusalem. Opposite the gate, several hundred metres along on the left in Derekh Shkhem (Nablus Road) is the ★ **Garden Tomb** (Monday to Saturday 8am–1pm and 3.30–5pm), which has come to be known as the Protestant Holy Sepulchre. The Garden Tomb was discovered in the late 19th century by General Gordon (of Khartoum fame) during a pilgrimage to the Holy City. Gordon reportedly observed the skull-like rock formations from his hotel window, which was just outside the Old City walls and deduced that this might be Calvary. When he discovered a tomb on the site he was convinced that he had found the true Holy Sepulchre. Gordon was reportedly depressed to find the Church of the Holy Sepulchre to be in the hands of Catholics, Orientals and Africans and no doubt the Garden Tomb appealed to his imperialistic sensibilities. In any event, the gardens set up here make for a pleasant and tranquil oasis amid the hubbub of East Jerusalem, regardless of the authenticity of the site.

Back along Sultan Suleiman, which runs parallel to the Old City walls and passes Herod's Gate, known as Sha'ar ha-Prakhim (Flowers Gate) in Hebrew, is the ★ **Rockefeller Museum** (Sunday to Thursday 10am–5pm, Friday and Saturday 10am–2pm). Opened in 1938, the museum contains an extensive collection of Middle East archaeology, the most important in Israel. In addition to the exhibits, the attractive architecture and elegant, outside pool are a major attraction.

Route 3

Mount of Olives and Mount Scopus

Garden of Gethsemane – Mount of Olives – Mount Scopus – Mormon University – Hebrew University – Ammunition Hill – American Colony Hotel – St George's Cathedral *See map on pages 14–15*

This tour is devoted to the mountain ridge east of and overlooking the Old City. The Mount of Olives is probably the most sacred site in Jerusalem outside of the Old City and it also offers a stirring view of the Temple Mount. The tour can be undertaken either on foot or by car. The distances involved are not great but can seem very long during the heat of the summer.

★★ **The Garden of Gethsemane** ㉘ (daily 8am–noon and 2.30–5pm) is located on the main highway to Jericho, Derekh Yerikho, as it winds its way beneath the eastern wall of the Old City. It was in this garden that it is believed that Christ prayed after the Last Supper before being betrayed by Judas Iscariot and arrested by the Romans. The major attraction of the garden is the olive trees, with splendidly twisted, gnarled barks that look as though they have witnessed the passing of millennia. It is only appropriate that the olive trees steal the show. After all, this is at the foot of the Mount of Olives and Gethsemane is derived from the Hebrew *Gat-shamna* which means olive press.

Gethsemane: Christ is led away and the olive trees

27

The garden stands in front of the **Church of All Nations** ㉙, also called the Basilica of the Agony. Built in 1924 by the Franciscans, the church's most conspicuous aspect is the large mosaic facade above the main entrance which depicts Christ mediating between God and the people. Originally the site of a Byzantine chapel it is popularly accepted that this was the part of the garden in which Christ was arrested and 'the rock of agony' enclosed in a grating shaped like a crown of thorns in the centre of the church is believed to be the very spot of the arrest.

Opposite the garden on the northern side is **Mary's Tomb** ㉚ (Monday to Saturday 6.30am–noon, 2–5pm). Tradition has it that Christ's mother is buried in the tomb on the right hand side of this candle-lit cave, which is part Byzantine and part Crusader and is today controlled by the Greek Orthodox church, though the Armenians, Copts and Syrian Orthodox churches all have their own altars. This is in fact believed to be a family mausoleum and halfway down the staircase on the right is the tomb of Mary's parents, Joachim and Anne, while on the left her husband Joseph is believed to be buried.

Mary's Tomb

From the garden, walk up the right-hand lane for several hundred metres to arrive at the ★★ **Church of St Mary Magdalene** ③. This is one of Jerusalem's most distinctive landmarks with its seven, delightfully proportioned, golden onion-shaped domes. The church, which claims to stand on part of the Garden of Gethsemane, was built in 1886 by Czar Alexander III. Unfortunately, the church has very limited opening hours (Tuesday and Thursday from 10–11.30am).

Further up the lane a path to the left leads to the **Church of Dominus Flevit** ③ (8–11.45am and 3–4.45pm). The existing church was only built by the Franciscans in 1955, on the site on the Mount of Olives where according to Luke 19:41 Christ wept for Jerusalem. Consequently the church, which was designed by the Franciscan Antonio Barluzzi and stands on the ruins of Byzantine and Crusader chapels, is shaped like a tear. There is a beautfiul view of the Dome of the Rock from the altar window.

· THE SANCTUARY OF THE ·
DOMINUS   FLEVIT
✠

Where Christ wept for Jerusalem

At the top of the hill, to the right in front of the Seven Arches Hotel is the ★★ **Mount of Olives Lookout** ③. This is the best and most popular vantage point from which to view the Temple Mount. There are usually several camels here with minders hoping to profit from tourists eager to take a brief camel ride.

Immediately in front of the lookout is the **Jewish Cemetery**. According to Jewish tradition, when the Messiah comes he will enter the Temple Mount through the Golden Gate, the walled-in gate which can clearly be seen opposite the Mount of Olives. The belief is that the Messiah will then construct a bridge of paper and a bridge of metal and the corpses buried on the Mount of Olives will be the first to return to life. Those who have faith will cross successfully on the bridge of paper, while those who do not will cross on the bridge of metal and fall to perdition in the valley below.

View from the Mount of Olives

There are several more churches in the Arab village of **E-Tur**, which straddles the ridge between the Mount of Olives and Mount Scopus. Opposite the beginning of Rub'a El-Adawiya, the main street through the village, is the **Church of Pater Noster** ③ (daily 8.30am–11.45am and 3–4.45pm). This Catholic church, built for the Carmelite sisters in 1868 by Princess de la Tour D'Auvergne of France, has attractive cloisters including a courtyard wall with the Lord's Prayer inscribed in 63 different languages. Also in the grounds of the church are the ruins of the **Eleona Church** built originally by Queen Helena and rebuilt by the Crusaders but destroyed after their defeat. It is believed that on this site Christ taught his disciples the Lord's Prayer and predicted the end of the world.

Church of Pater Noster

On the right at the start of Rub'a El-Adawiya is the small octagonal **Chapel of the Ascension** , which is in fact a mosque. Initially built as a church in the 4th century and converted to a mosque in 1187 after the defeat of the Crusaders, Catholics believe that this was the site of Christ's ascension. However, the Russian Orthodox church begs to differ claiming that its **Church of the Ascension**, down the lane to the east, with its distinctive high bell tower, is the real site of the ascension.

Visiting pilgrim

Heading northwards to Mount Scopus, the **Augusta Victoria Hospital** on the right, which also has a distinctively high tower, was originally built by Germans as a hospice but has served as a hospital for the past 50 years. The road passes through a copse of pine trees and on the right is a superb view of the Judean Desert, billowing serenely into the distance, and in the clearer air of the winter the Mountains of Moab in Jordan can be seen beyond. Further along, on a clear day, it is also possible to see the Dead Sea.

A new road on the left leads down to the ★ **Jerusalem Centre for Near Eastern Studies – Brigham Young University** ㊱ known locally as the Mormon University. The construction of this extremely attractive campus and college building, built into the hillside on eight levels, was fiercely opposed by orthodox Jews when it was being erected during the 1980s. But in the interests of pluralism, the Mormons from Salt Lake City, Utah, were allowed to go ahead with their project providing no missionary activity takes place in Israel. Students, who come to Jerusalem for semester-long courses, are warned that they will be sent home if they indulge in any proselytising activi-

29

Chapel of the Ascension

ties. From Tuesday to Friday there are tours in English at 10.30 am, 11.30am, 2.30pm and 3.30pm around the campus which commands a remarkable view of the Old City. It also has exceptionally pleasant gardens including a 2,000-year-old olive tree that was transplanted from the Galilee hills.

To the north of the Mormon campus is the ★ **Hebrew University**'s ❸ humanities and social sciences campus. This sprawling, fortress-like structure is more attractive than it first seems and within are some attractive gardens. Also worth seeing is the amphitheatre, which is on the left past the junction of Martin Buber and Shomrei ha-Har. The amphitheatre, built in 1926 for the University's inauguration, offers a splendid panorama of the desert behind the stage. From 1948 to 1967 the University was cut off from Jewish west Jerusalem and soldiers were escorted up once a month by the UN to guard the deserted buildings. During the 1970s, the modern campus was built. There are daily tours in English leaving from the Sherman Administration Building, which is opposite the Botanical Gardens in the northwest corner of the campus. Particularly attractive is the Hecht Synagogue with its view of the Old City.

The summit of **Mount Scopus** is 830 metres (2,720ft) high and at about 100 metres above the Old City, the heights dominate ancient Jerusalem. No wonder that the dozens of different powers throughout history that have attacked the Holy City have amassed their forces and attacked from here in the north.

To the northwest of the University, along Shderot Churchill, is **Hadassah Hospital** which like the University was cut off from 1948 to 1967. And, just as the University built a new campus at Givat Ram in the west of the city (today the science campus), so the Hospital built a

View from Mount Scopus

new medical centre in Ein Kerem. Adjacent to the hospital is the **British Military Cemetery**, whose neat rows of graves are for the soldiers who fell here in World War I and through to the end of the British Mandate in 1948.

Past the Hyatt Regency Hotel, which dominates the hillside along Aharon Katsir Street, there is a complex of government offices on the south side of Shderot ha-Universita ha-Ivrit which includes the national police headquarters. To the south of these offices is **Sheikh Jarah**, the most exclusive neighbourhood in East Jerusalem where the city's wealthiest Arabs live.

On the far side of Derekh ha-Shalom, the main highway heading north out of the city, and opposite the police headquarters, is a small park leading to **Ammunition Hill** ❸❽ (Givat ha-Takhmoshet) (Sunday to Thursday 9am– 4pm, Friday 9am–1pm). Between 1948 and 1967 this hill marked the most forward fortifications of the Jordanian Army. Captured by the Israelis during the Six Day War, the hill was subsequently dedicated as a monument to the Israeli soldiers who fell in battle, and a small museum tells their sad story.

Ammunition Hill

Derekh ha-Shalom (literally meaning the peace highway) runs southward along the line on which a large wall divided the city between 1948 and 1967. A left turn into Van Paassen leads to the **American Colony Hotel**, the city's oldest hotel, established in the late 19th century by the Spafford family, American Presbyterians who greeted such travellers as Mark Twain and Herman Melville and still manage the place. The hotel has always had a trendy popularity, especially with the foreign press corps, because of its 'neutral' location between the Jewish and Arab parts of the city.

31

New Orient House

On the next street south of the hotel, Abu Ubaida, is **New Orient House**, which has emerged in recent years as quasi-Palestinian government building in East Jerusalem. Foreign diplomats and visiting overseas government ministers will sometimes hold talks here with Palestinian officials, despite Israeli government protests.

At the corner of Abu Ubaida and Derekh Shkhem is the **Tomb of the Kings** ❸❾ (Monday to Saturday 8am–12.30pm and 2–5pm). While this well preserved 1st-century tomb may interest archaeology experts, it has long been disproven that any kings are actually buried here.

On the fork junction to the south of the tombs is **St George's Cathedral** ❹⓪, the seat of the Anglican Bishop of Jerusalem and the Middle East. Completed in 1910, this was so to speak an attempt to build England in Jerusalem's arid and rugged terrain. The cathedral complex has attractive gardens and an English-style guest house as well as a school.

St George's Cathedral

Studies in Me'a She'arim

Route 4

The New City

Me'a She'arim – The Russian Compound – Downtown Jerusalem – Rekhavya – Jerusalem Theatre – German Colony *See map on pages 14–15*

The notion of the New City is something of an anachronistic term kept alive by visitors from overseas. Locals rarely use the term, which once referred to the new neighbourhoods, mainly Jewish, being built to the west of the Old City. Some of those new neighbourhoods were built 130 years ago. This area also contains the commercial and entertainment heart of the city, often referred to as the centre of town. Once again, modest dress is required for touring the ultra-orthodox Jewish quarter of Me'a She'arim.

Orthodox youngsters

★★ **Me'a She'arim** was founded in 1874 by ultra-orthodox Jews from Central and Eastern Europe and not very much has changed since then. The black garb of the men is 17th-century European, and the lifestyle resembles that of the Amish in Pennsylvania. The banners urging women to dress and behave modestly should be taken very seriously and it is not advisable for men and women to even hold hands. Cameras and radios are forbidden on the Sabbath. Local men can be very aggressive and even spit and throw stones if these rules are ignored.

Me'a She'arim is the name of the main street of the quarter. It literally means 'one hundred gates' and is taken from a quote in Genesis about Isaac receiving a one hundred fold return for the seeds that he planted. Others claim that the name refers to the one hundred entrances that existed when the quarter was walled in its formative years.

The main street stretches westwards from the junction with Shivtei Yisrael. On the corner is the Ministry of Education building, formerly the Italian Hospital, built in 1912 in the medieval Italian style with a distinctive high square tower. Me'a She'arim itself is also distinctly medieval. Off the side streets are entrances to courtyards around which the neighbourhood's homes are built. The ultra-orthodox women, usually with a very large brood to care for, jealously guard their privacy, so be discreet when peeping into these courtyards.

On the right by the first junction of Me'a She'arim is the **Toldot Aharon Yeshiva**. Such institutions are the soul of the neighbourhood because ultra-orthodox men exist in order to study and interpret the Old Testament. The young boys have pale skin (and usually glasses) because of the intense, indoor life of studying that they lead. Active pursuits are frowned upon as a Hellenistic influence.

Toldot Aharon Yeshiva

For the most part, Me'a Shearim is a place to stroll through and enjoy the exotic ethnic experience. There are some excellent stores in the main street for the purchase of Judaica. Midway along Me'a She'arim, Baharan on the left is a narrow road leading up into Etyopya Street. This delightful narrow lane, much more serene than the frenetic ultra-orthodox neighbourhood, contains some of the city's most expensive homes, and is dominated by the **Ethiopian Church** on the left. Completed in 1906 this is the largest Ethiopian church in Israel.

33

Delightful Etyopya Street

Etyopya Street leads into Ha-Nevi'im (the street of the Prophets), which also contains some of the city's grand 19th-century houses with lush gardens. Straight across Ha-Nevi'im is Ha'Rav Kook and down on the right of this street is **Beit Tikho** ❹, which is administered by the Israel Museum and exhibits the paintings of Jerusalem's foremost landscape artist Anna Tikho. Also on display are her husband's collection of Chanukiot (candle holders used during the Jewish festival of Chanukah). This museum is located in the former home of the Tichos, an impressive large house with a pleasant garden café and restaurant.

The next turning on the right along Ha-Nevi'im, Monbaz, leads into the ★ **Russian Compound**. This quarter was given by the Ottomans as a gift to the Czar in 1853 and subsequently buildings were constructed to house Russian pilgrims visiting the Holy City. Most of the buildings have been sold to the Israeli government, and Monbaz and Heleni ha-Malka contain dozens of pubs and bars making this the place to be from midnight onwards. The Russian presence remains, however, in the form of the **Holy Trinity Cathedral** ❷, an impressive, characteristically Slavic structure with white walls and a green roof, which stands at the junction of Zmora and Kheshin.

Holy Trinity Cathedral

Kheshin leads down to **Jaffa Road** (Yafo Road), the main thoroughfare through the New City. Just along Yafo to the left is the impressive new **Jerusalem Municipality Building** which was completed in 1993, while to the right is the centre of town. To the south of Yafo is ★ **Nahlat Shiva**. Built in 1869, it is one of the oldest neighbourhoods outside the Old City. Several of the streets – Rivlin and Salomon – were recently pedestrianised and this is a pleasant place to stroll in the evening, and there are a large number of restaurants to choose from.

Dining in Nahlat Shiva

★ **Ben Yehuda ㊸**, however, in the section leading between Yafo Road and Ha-Melekh George, is the heart of the city's commercial and café life. Together with its side streets, this area is bustling with life from mid-morning until after midnight. The cafés' outdoor tables are packed with people, both locals and tourists, who enjoy watching the world go by. Ben Yehuda leads uphill to Ha-Melekh George, one of the city's major north-south arteries. In front of the Hamashbir department store at the junction is the rather odd looking **Talitha Kumi** wall with a clock preserved from a 19th-century school which once stood on the site. Several hundred metres down Hillel on the left is the **Italian Synagogue and Museum** (Sunday and Tuesday 10am–1pm, Wednesday 4–7pm), an early 18th-century synagogue from near Venice which was brought to Jerusalem in 1952.

The **Ministry of Tourism** building on Ha-Melekh George, between Be'eri and Shatz, acted as the Knesset (parliament) during the early years of the state. There is a computer terminal offering tourist information near the building's front entrance. Further along on the right is the **Jewish Agency** building which was the quasi-Jewish government during the period of the British mandate. On the left hand side of the street is **Independence Park** (Ha-Atsmaut Garden), a pleasant expanse of green in the midst of the city, which like so many other areas of parkland in Jerusalem was kept out of the hands of property developers by the determined bullying of Austrian-born Teddy Kollek, who served as the city's mayor from 1965 to 1993 and imposed his Viennese sense of aesthetics and elegance on the city.

Independence Park and the Sheraton Plaza

Near the junction with Agron, opposite the huge concrete block of the Sheraton Plaza, is the **Jerusalem Great Synagogue ㊹**, a huge building, dedicated in 1983, whose construction was fiercely opposed by Mr Kollek. To the east of Ha-Melekh George, at this point, is Rekhavya, a salubrious 'garden suburb' built in the first half of the 20th century, which has stylish houses in narrow leafy lanes such as Elkharizi, the first turning on the right off Ramban. **Kikar Tsarfat** (French Square) with the distinguished

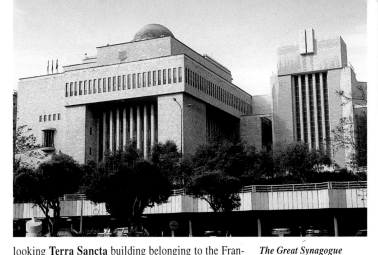

looking **Terra Sancta** building belonging to the Franciscans on its southern side is not quite the ordinary looking city junction that it seems. It straddles the continental divide – in other words, water running down Ben Maimon to the west would theoretically reach the Mediterranean and Atlantic Oceans, while to the east water would run to the Great Syrian African rift valley.

On the corner of Balfour and Smolenskin, just to the south west of Kikar Tsarfat, is the Prime Minister's Residence. There is nearly always some kind of demonstration going on outside, watched over by a heavy police presence.

Balfour leads into Jabotinski and to the west along that road is the **President's Residence**, and just past it at the junction of Ha-Palmakh and Ha-Nasi is the **Islamic Art Museum** ⑮ (Saturday to Thursday 8am–4pm) which houses exhibits of ceramics, tapestry, calligraphy, jewellery and other aesthetic skills from Islamic countries throughout the world.

Along Chopin is the **Jerusalem Centre for the Performing Arts** ⑯, a complex that includes the Jerusalem Theatre and the Henry Crown Hall, home of the Jerusalem Symphony Orchestra. The neighbourhood of **Talbiya** to the east is also a delightful collection of leafy, tastefully affluent homes and gardens.

From the theatre, Dubnov and its extension Graetz lead down to **Emek Refaim**, the main road leading through the fashionable **German Colony** (Ha-Moshava ha-Germanit), which takes its name from the German Templars who founded the neighbourhood in 1873 and still maintain a nunnery on Lloyd George Street. Both the German Colony and the adjacent quarter of **Baq'a** to the east contain narrow lanes and stylish, modestly proportioned Arab houses and gardens.

The Great Synagogue

35

Jerusalem Centre for the Peforming Arts

In the German Colony

Route 5

South of the City

East Talpiyot Promenade – Yemin Moshe – Mamila – New Gate *See map on pages 14–15*

This walk starts from the East Talpiyot Promenade with its fine view of the Old City and the Dead Sea valley and leads northwards (via an unattractive industrial area) through the twee alleyways of Yemin Moshe to the Old City. Overall, the route shows the tasteful and elegant manner in which Jerusalem has been preserved and developed in the past few decades.

★★ **The East Talpiyot Promenade** ㉗ to the south of the city is located on a ridge to the west of **Government House (Armon ha-Natsiv)**, completed in 1931 as the residence and administrative building for the British High Commissioner during the Mandate period and taken over in 1948 by the United Nations as its headquarters for Middle East operations. This is also known as the **Hill of Evil Counsel**, not because of anything against even the British or the UN, but because Christians believe that the house of Caiaphas, the high priest who allegedly paid Judas to betray Christ, was here.

In any event, the view from the recently built Haas Promenade is extraordinary. Not only can the Old City be seen in all its glory but in the foreground the Kidron Valley leads the eye past Arab villages and down to the Judean Desert and Dead Sea, though the heat haze in the summer blocks out this part of the panorama.

Aspects of the East Talpiyot Promenade

The view can also be enjoyed from the **Sherover Walkway** ㉘ which leads north from the Promenade, pass-

ing through a delightfully landscaped park and gardens on the slopes of the hill. The Walkway skirts the St Clair Monastery and reaches **Abu Tor**, a mixed Jewish and Arab neighbourhood named after a Muslim warrior who joined forces with Saladin to help defeat the Crusaders.

The main road through Abu Tor, Derekh Khevron, runs northward. To the left at the junction with David Remez is the **Railway Station** built by the Ottoman Turks in 1892. The link between Jaffa and Jerusalem was the first railway line in Palestine, but today its importance has declined. There is one train a day and it takes several hours to reach Tel Aviv compared to 45 minutes by bus. But the rail route is worth taking for its scenic beauty especially the section through the Sorek Valley to the west of Jerusalem (*see Excursion 1, page 50*).

The Khan Theatre

Opposite the station is the **Khan Theatre** , a 19th-century warehouse for storing rail cargo which has been converted into a theatre usually showing fringe productions. Behind the theatre is **St Andrew's Church** ⑩, which can be reached either from the junction of David Remez and David ha-Melekh, or from Derekh Khevron. Owned by the Church of Scotland, St Andrew's Church was built in 1927 to celebrate the British capture of the Holy Land 10 years earlier. This is the only Calvinist church in Jerusalem and attached to it is a guest house which, while not serving kippers, does have mince pies and mulled wine at Christmas. Adjacent to the church is West Jerusalem's **British Consulate**.

House of Quality

The House of Quality ㉛ on Derekh Khevron just to the east of the church is a converted eye hospital which contains workshops and stores with goods made by local artists. From the building opposite a cable pulley **stretching** across to **Mount Zion** has been preserved to recall the struggle to link up with Jewish forces cut off during the War of Independence in 1948.

Further along Derekh Khevron the **Cinematheque** on the right is a trendy cinema that shows the best of world movies and a selection of golden oldies. It is also the focus for the Jerusalem International Film Festival each June. The Cinematheque's restaurant offers an excellent view of Mount Zion and the **Hinnom Valley**. At night the belfry of the Church of the Dormition on Mount Zion looks eerily like a German soldier wearing a helmet.

The Hinnom Valley

It is hard to believe that the picturesque Hinnom Valley is historically associated with hell. In biblical times the false God Moloch was believed to have performed child sacrifices here.

Over the footbridge and leading back to the entrance of St Andrew's Church there are several parks. **The Liberty Bell Park** (Ha-Pa'amon) on the west side of David

Exploring Liberty Bell Park

Montefiore's Windmill

Fireworks at Sultan's Pool

ha-Melekh is a wonderful place to take kids. There are playgrounds, sports areas, a skating rink, trampolines, a puppet theatre in a railway carriage and much more, as well as lawns and benches. The park takes its name from a replica of the Liberty Bell presented to Jerusalem by Philadelphia in honour of the US Bicentennial in 1976. On the other side of David ha-Melekh is the attractive Bloomfield Garden.

At the northern end of the park is the **Laromme Hotel**. Completed in 1980, the hotel has come to challenge the nearby **King David** (several hundred metres up David ha-Melekh) as the city's leading establishment. The Laromme has a light, airy, modern atmosphere, while the King David, which was only built in the 1930s, oozes a solid, staid, old-world ambiance.

Opposite the Laromme Hotel, Shderot Blumfield leads by a colourful tulip garden to ★ **Yemin Moshe**. The lower section of this neighbourhood on the right, **Mishkenot Sha'ananim** (Dwellings of Tranquillity) was the first Jewish housing in Jerusalem outside of the Old City when it was built in 1860. So fearful were the Jews to live outside of the walls that it took 10 years before anybody could be persuaded to move out here. The rest of the quarter was built in 1890.

The focal point of Yemin Moshe is **Montefiore's Windmill 52**, a famous Jerusalem landmark. The windmill was built in 1858 to provide a livelihood for the people of Mishkenot Sha'ananim but was never used. Inside is a museum (Sunday to Thursday 8.30am–4.30pm, Friday 9am–1pm, closed Saturday) which explains the history of this neighbourhood. Next to the windmill is a replica of the coach in which a British philanthropist, Moses Montefiore, who initiated and funded Mishkenot Sha'ananim,

travelled to the Holy Land. The original coach was mysteriously burned in the 1980s.

Today Yemin Moshe is just about the city's most expensive neighbourhood, while Mishkenot Sha'ananim is used as a municipal guest house for visiting artists. Seeing the expensive homes, and delightfully renovated alleyways, it is hard to believe that before the Six Day War in 1967 these were some of the city's worst slums because of their precarious location next to the border with Jordan.

Beneath Yemin Moshe is the **Sultan's Pool Amphitheatre ㊳**. In the summer months when there are regular concerts, both classical and popular, it is worth attending a performance here. Romantically located beneath the walls of the Old City there can be few venues in the world to compare with this. Historically this was a reservoir built by Suleiman to contain run-off water during the winter.

To the right of Dror Eli'el is **Khutsot ha-Yotser**, a collection of upmarket souvenir shops and art galleries. In the summer there is a prestigious arts and crafts fair here. Emile Botta Street, leading back westwards, has some of the city's most stylish buildings, including the **French Consulate** and further up the **Pontifical Biblical Institute**. On the left, at the junction with Dvaid ha-Melekh, is the **King David Hotel**, which over the decades has housed dozens of world leaders and celebrities. But the hotel's most famous episode was when it served as the British Army headquarters in the last years of the mandate and an entire wing was blown up by the right-wing Jewish underground, killing 50 people. On the far side of the junction is the **YMCA**, with its distinctive tower, designed in the 1930s by Shreve, Lamb and Harman, the American architects who designed the Empire State Building.

YMCA building

Going northwards down David ha-Melekh there are many upmarket art galleries and Judaica stores as well the campus of the **Hebrew Union College**, the Israeli headquarters of the American-based world Jewish reform movement (the World Union for Progressive Judaism). Despite the flourishing campus, Reform Judaism as well as other non-orthodox movements such as the Conservative movement, have failed to take root in Israel, both legally because the orthodox Jews maintain monopolistic jurisdiction over marriage and death, and popularly, because only small numbers of secular Jews have joined congregations.

Hebrew Union College

David ha-Melekh leads down to Taxation Square (Kikar ha-Mekhes). On the left is the **Taxation Museum ㊴** (Sunday and Tuesday 9am–noon), which tells the story of local taxation since Ottoman times. On the right of the intersection is **Mamila**. Once a commercial quarter filled with workshops and garages, this entire neighbourhood

New Gate

was razed to make way for a new entity that would link the New City with the Old City. The new Mamila includes luxury apartments and hotels, and a large underground car park. One of the few buildings that was not destroyed was the Catholic orphanage of **St Vincent de Paul**, which majestically overlooks the new development.

Shlomo ha-Melekh leads up to the Old City walls and straight over the intersection along Ha-Tsankhanim on the right is the **New Gate**. This, as the name implies, is the newest entrance to the Old City. It was cut open in 1889 to provide access between the Christian Quarter and the Christian institutions within the vicinity of the Old City.

Notre Dame de France

The nearest and most conspicuous of these is the **Notre Dame de France** ⑤⑤, a hospice opposite the New Gate which is housed in a grandiose, palatial building constructed in 1887 for pilgrims. Since its refurbishment in the 1970s, Notre Dame has become one of Jerusalem's most luxurious hotels, and it also has a very highly regarded French restaurant.

The story of Notre Dame highlights the complex political realities of modern Jerusalem. Founded and originally owned by the French Assumptionist Catholic order, the building was badly damaged by shelling during the Six Day War in 1967. The Assumptionists subsequently sold the building to the Hebrew University. However, the Vatican was furious that such an important and strategically located Christian property had been sold to non-Catholics without Papal approval. Charging that such a deed was against Canon law, the Vatican sued for negation of contract in the Israeli secular courts. The matter was settled expediently out of court as the Israeli government, not wishing to alienate the Vatican, agreed to sell the building back to the Vatican.

Route 6

West of the City

Makhane Yehuda – Knesset – Israel Museum – Monastery of the Cross – Botanical Gardens *See map on pages 14–15*

Starting at the bustling Makhane Yehuda market and narrow alleyways of Nakhlaot, this route reaches the open spaces of Sacher Park. In this pleasantly green part of the city, immediately west of the centre, lie Jerusalem's most important cultural and political institutions, including the buildings of government, the Supreme Court and the Knesset (parliament). Nearby is the Israel Museum, whose exhibits include the Dead Sea Scrolls, and several other museums worth visiting. To the south is the Monastery of the Cross, where the wood for Christ's crucifix is believed to have been taken from, while the Botanical Gardens is beneath the Hebrew University's Givat Ram campus.

The heart of ★ **Makhane Yehuda market** ❺, a five-minute walk eastwards along Yafo from the Central Bus Station, runs along a covered passageway between Yafo and Agripas streets. The market is famous for its vociferous vendors, often expressing right-wing political opinions, and its colourful array of food products, especially fresh fruit and vegetables, pickles, dried fruits and nuts and cheeses. The freshest choice is offered early in the morning, while the best bargains can be found on Friday afternoon before the Sabbath when stallholders will virtually give perishable items away. At any time this is the cheapest place in town to buy food.

Makhane Yehuda market scenes

The market was established in 1887 and a fascinating sight, rarely seen even by locals because of the narrowness of Yafo street at the northern end of the market, is one of the world's strangest clocks. Located above a synagogue opposite the entrance to the market, it has a semi-circular sundial, a conventional clock, and a clock which indicates the amount of time until the next Jewish prayers (Jews pray three time a day – just after sunrise, just before sunset and just after sunset).

Agripas street also has many market stalls and stores but is most famous for its eateries, especially steak houses serving grilled meats. On the south side of Agripas is Nakhla'ot, a crumbling but fashionable neighbourhood built at the end of the 19th century which has been undergoing gentrification. Shilo street, running immediately south of the market, characterises this phenomenon with slums alongside very expensive properties.

Betsal'el runs down westwards to Sacher Park, the city's largest park and a favourite expanse of grass for soccer players. Above the park is the ★ **Supreme Court** ⑰, (Sunday to Thursday 8.30am–2.30pm). Completed in 1992, this impressive building uses light, shade and glass to great effect. The Supreme Court justices comprise the highest court in the land and have the power to interpret Knesset laws.

To the west of the court is the **Wohl Rose Park** which is at its blooming best in the early spring and late autumn. The park is said to have different 450 species of rose. The **Bank of Israel** and the **Prime Minister's Office** are to the west of the park while ★ **The Knesset** ⑱, Israel's parliament building (Monday to Wednesday during debates and Sunday and Thursday 8.30am–2.30pm for guided tours; admittance only on presentation of a passport), can be reached south along Kaplan and left into Rothschild. The centrepiece of the building, opened in 1966, is a 120-member chamber where parliamentary debates take place between the representatives elected every four years by proportional representation. The reception area contains a large tapestry of Jewish history designed by the artist Marc Chagall. Peculiarly, the Knesset chamber is downstairs from the entrance. This is because the original plan for the building called for the entrance to be located on the lower elevation of the southern side. But security officials pointed out prior to the opening in 1966 that Jordanian artillery in the West Bank several kilometres to the north could easily shell the entrance plaza. Opposite the existing entrance on the northern side is a **Menora** (candelabra), a gift from the British government.

Further south along Kaplan and across the intersection at Ruppin is the entrance to the ★★★ **Israel Museum** ⑲ (Sunday, Monday, Wednesday and Thursday 10am–5pm, Tuesday 4–10pm, Friday 10am–2pm, Saturday 10am–4pm). This is one of the world's foremost museums with famous collections of archaeology, art and Jewish ethnography. The most famous exhibit, the Dead Sea Scrolls, are contained in a separate distinctive white, dome-shaped building – **the Shrine of the Book** ⑳ – just inside the ticket office. Frankly, the romantic story of their discovery by a Bedouin boy and the fact that this is the oldest known copy of the Old Testament, is far more exciting than the actual pieces of tattered parchment. The main part of the Museum is strongest on local archaeology as well as Torah scrolls and items of Judaica collected from the Diaspora including entire reconstructions of synagogues from Italy and Poland. There is also an excellent collection of 19th- and 20th-century French art and the Museum has a good Youth Wing to entertain the children.

42

Opposite the Israel Museum is the recently opened **Bible Lands Museum** ❻❶ (Sunday, Monday, Tuesday and Thursday 9.30am–5.30pm, Wednesday 1.30–9.30pm, Friday 9.30am–2pm and Saturday 11am–3pm). This museum contains collections of archaeological artifacts from the Mediterranean and Middle Eastern civilisations that laid the foundations for the Judeo-Christian heritage.

Another popular museum to the north along Ruppin or Shderot ha-Muze'onim is the **Science Museum** ❻❷ (Monday, Wednesday and Thursday 10am–6pm, Tuesday 10am–8pm, Friday 10am–1pm and Saturday 10am–3pm), which has hands-on exhibits for children of all ages.

The Science Museum

The rugged hillside park with olive trees to the southeast of the Israel Museum's entrance is the **Valley of the Cross**, from where it is believed the tree was cut down for the wood on which Christ was crucified. Legend has it that this was no ordinary tree, but three intertwined trees (a cedar, olive and pomegranate) planted by Lot, Abraham's nephew, after he was saved from the destruction of Sodom.

★ **The Monastery of the Holy Cross** ❻❸ (Monday to Saturday 9.30am–5pm, Friday 9am–1.30pm, closed Sunday) is believed to be located on the very site on which these three trees grew. This large, fortress-like monastery dates back to 313, but the original building was destroyed by the Persians in 614. It was rebuilt by Georgian monks immediately afterwards but razed again in 1009 and rebuilt shortly afterwards. The Georgian national poet Shoda Rustavelli is buried here and the monastery remained in the hands of the Georgian Orthodox church until entrusted to the Greek Orthodox Patriarchate of Jerusalem in 1840.

Monastery of the Holy Cross

South of the monastery, turn right along Yehoshua Yevin to Zalman Shne'ur, and the entrance to the **Botanical Gardens** is by the junction with Betsal'el Bazak. This is a small-scale but attractive garden with flora from around the world. Near the southern entrance is a lake with a café and restaurant at its side.

The Botanical Gardens

From the northern entrance to the gardens, a road leads up to the **Hebrew University's Givat Ram Campus**. Established here in the 1950s when the Mount Scopus campus was cut off from West Jerusalem, the campus contains the science faculties of the University as well as the **Jewish National and University Library** ❻❹ (Sunday to Thursday 9am–5pm, Friday 9am–noon, closed Saturday) one of the world's largest libraries with the biggest collection of books relating to Judaism and Jewish culture. Permanent exhibits include the original manuscripts on which Albert Einstein first scribbled his Theory of Relativity. Also on campus is the **Open Eye Science Centre** (Sunday to Friday 9am–1pm and Saturday 10am–3pm) which has hands-on science exhibits designed for children.

Route 7

Mount Herzl and Malha

Yad Vashem – Har Herzl Cemetery – Second Temple Model – Kanion (Shopping Mall) – Biblical Zoo – Ein Yael Living Museum *See map on pages 14–15*

The Yad Vashem Holocaust Memorial and Museum is a harrowing reminder of man's potential for cruelty in general and the not so distant suffering of the Jewish people prior to the establishment of Israel. Nearby the Har Herzl Cemetery contains the graves of the country's former leaders, including Yitzhak Rabin who was assassinated in 1995. No less moving are the graves of hundreds of less illustrious soldiers who have also paid the ultimate price in the Israel-Arab conflict.

In contrast to the sombreness of Har Herzl, the Malkha Valley several kilometres to the south is a place for relaxation. In addition to a large shopping mall and the city's soccer stadium, the Biblical Zoo and the Ein Yael Living Museum are fun places to take the kids.

★★ Yad Vashem, the Holocaust Memorial and Museum ❻❺ (Sunday to Thursday 9am–5pm, Friday 9am–2pm, closed Saturday), a government institution founded in order to commemorate and research the Holocaust, is located on the Hill of Remembrance overlooking the Jerusalem Forest to the west of the city. When the pine forest was first established, 6 million trees were planted to represent those Jews who perished in the Holocaust. There are more trees, just a few dozen, along the entrance promenade to the Museum which is called the Avenue of the Righteous Gentiles. Each tree here represents non-Jews,

*Yad Vashem,
the Holocaust Memorial*

who had the rare courage to risk their own lives to save Jews, and this provides an optimistic note before the grim narrative of barbarity that the Museum recalls. The Museum itself uses simple enlarged black and white photographs, newspaper cuttings and documentary narrative to recount the rise of Nazism and the subsequent extermination of the Jews during World War II.

The Museum attempts to lend a sense of individual horror to the vast statistics surrounding the Holocaust. Therefore, at the end of the Museum is the Hall of Remembrance, which has tried to collect the actual names and biographical details of all those who died. However, because entire communities were annihilated with barely a survivor, only 3 million names have so far been recorded. The Art Exhibition above the Museum is another tangible way in which the victims have been remembered. Especially heart rending are some of the colourful, joyful drawings of small children etched shortly before they were gassed in Auschwitz and Belsen.

Where grief is permanent

Other sites at Yad Vashem include a memorial chamber used for religious ceremonies with the names of the 22 concentration camps engraved in black basalt rock. Up the stairs on the left near the entrance is a moving memorial to the 1½ million children who were killed in the Holocaust. It comprises a dark corridor in which lights and mirrors evocatively create thousands of small lights symbolising the lives that were snuffed out. Beneath the complex to the west is the Valley of the Lost Communities, where carved on large rocks are the names of 5,000 Jewish communities from France to Russia which were decimated. Yad Vashem also has the world's largest research and archives department on Holocaust-related topics.

4

To the right at the end of Ha-Zikaron is a large red, round work of art representing the sunset. Before modern times when the precise times of the sunset were not published in the newspapers, the city's orthodox Jews and Muslims would come to this western point of the city so that they could say their evening prayers immediately after the setting of the sun.

On the left at the end of Ha-Zikaron is the entrance to the **Mount (Har) Herzl Military Cemetery**. This cemetery not only contains the graves of hundreds of soldiers who have fallen in the country's wars, and most of the nation's former presidents and prime ministers, but also the remains of many architects of the state including Theodore Herzl, the founder of modern political Zionism. The **Herzl Museum** ⑥ to the left of the entrance (Sunday to Thursday 9am–5pm , Friday 9am–1pm, closed Saturday) has a collection of the Viennese journalist's former belongings.

Herzl Military Cemetery

Model of the Second Temple

But in the light of recent history, the most eye-catching and visited grave on Har Herzl, is the simple black-and-white tombstone near the entrance, of Yitzhak Rabin, the former Prime Minister, who was murdered in 1995, less than a year after being awarded the Nobel Peace Prize. Rabin, a former army chief who led Israel to a stunningly swift victory in the Six Day War and re-united Jerusalem, was gunned down by a right-wing opponent.

Opposite the entrance to the cemetery is Ha-Rav Uziel, which leads several kilometres southwards through the religious residential district of Bayit Va-Gan to the ★ **Model of the Second Temple 67** (Sunday to Thursday 8am–9pm, Friday and Saturday 8am–5pm). To save walking, it is possible to take bus number 21 from the start of Ha-Rav Uziel to the model which is located beneath the Holyland Hotel. This impressive 1:50 scale model of Jerusalem as it was in 66AD at the start of the Jewish revolt conveys just how vast the Second Temple complex really was.

The road leads down to the Malkha Valley which, until it was swallowed up in the early 1990s by Jerusalem's urban sprawl, was a pleasant, pastoral valley beneath the picturesque village of Malkha. Today Malkha's leisure facilities include **Teddy Stadium**, an attractive 12,000-seater soccer stadium which is the home of Betar Jerusalem, one of the country's leading teams. Adjacent to the stadium is the **Jerusalem Kanyon** (Shopping Mall), a shopping and entertainment complex with stores, restaurants, cafés and cinemas. Though this mall could be anywhere in the world, the convenience and the air-conditioning (or heating) can make this a comfortable place to spend some time.

Jerusalem Kanyon

The road running east of the Kanyon leads to the ★ **Biblical Zoo (Tisch Family Zoological Gardens) 68** (Sunday to Thursday 9am–5pm, Friday 9am–2pm and Saturday 10am–4pm). The zoo, which was only opened in 1993 and is attractively landscaped into the hillside, contains the animals mentioned in the Bible with the relevant quotations. Sadly, or perhaps thankfully, many of the animals which inhabited the region in biblical times such as lions, bears and crocodiles, are now extinct. There are lots of other animals, too, including rare birds and reptiles and there is a special children's section for riding ponies etc.

The **Ein Yael Living Museum 69** (9.30am–4.30pm; hands-on activities only on Saturdays, public holidays and throughout August) can be reached along the valley from the Kanyon. This museum has re-created a biblical village out of the archaeological remains of a real settlement and offers a 'hands-on' biblical experience by enabling visitors to create their own mosaics, harvest crops as if they were farmers living 2,000 years ago, practise ancient crafts and participate in archaeological digs.

Opposite: the Bedouin look

Excursion 1

Ein Kerem and the Jerusalem Hills

Ein Kerem – Chagall Windows – Sorek Caves – Beit Guvrin *See map on page 48*

A host at Ein Kerem

In addition to being a picturesque village worth visiting for its rural charm, Ein Kerem is popular with Christian pilgrims and it is believed that John the Baptist was born here, and that it was also here when visiting John's parents that the Archangel Gabriel told Mary that she would bear the Messiah. The large number of churches in the village and the lush, surrounding hillside forests give Ein Kerem the atmosphere of a European village. Ein Kerem's expensive houses are especially sought after by artists, who are inspired by the local vineyards and olive groves on the terraced hillsides. Nearby is Hadassa Hospital with its exquisite windows by Marc Chagall depicting the 12 tribes. The Sorek Valley to the west of Ein Kerem has delightful countryside and the unusual geological formations in the Sorek Caves are well worth seeing. There is also an interesting variety of man-made caves to the south west in Beit Guvrin. Ein Kerem can be reached on bus 17, Hadassah Hospital on bus 19, but a car is needed for the Sorek Cave and Beit Guvrin.

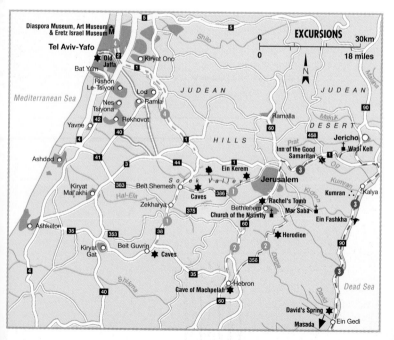

★★ **Ein Kerem** is a 20-minute car ride from the city centre along Highway 386. Just before the village square there is a small turning on the right called Ha-Sha'ar which leads to the **Church of St John the Baptist** (daily 8am–noon, 2.30–4pm). Built by the Franciscans in 1674 on the ruins of a Byzantine chapel, it is believed that John himself was born in the grotto beneath the church. In the grotto there are bas-reliefs depicting the Baptist's life and a marble slab containing the inscription 'Hic Praecursor Domini natus est – here the precursor of the Lord was born'. In the northern chapel there are mosaics from the original Byzantine chapel.

Church of St John the Baptist

On the other side of the main street, along Ha-Ma'ayan to the left of the junction with Madregot ha-Bikur (stairs of the Visitation) by an abandoned mosque, is the spring from which the village takes its name – Ein Kerem is Hebrew for 'Spring of the Vineyard'. On the wall by the spring is a quotation from Isaiah 'every one that is thirsty come for water'. **The Church of the Visitation** (daily 9am–noon, 2.30–5pm) at the top of the stairs also belongs to the Franciscans, though this is a more contemporary institution built only in 1956. On the front wall is a colourful mosaic depicting Mary in Ein Kerem as related in the book of Luke. According to tradition the summer house of Zacharia and Elizabeth stood on this site and when Mary was visiting them she was told by the Archangel Gabriel that she had been chosen to give birth to Christ. The lower floor of the church contains a cistern and an alcove where it is said that John hid from the Roman soldiers. The upper storey contains the apse of a Crusader church.

At the top of the hill is the **Russian Church of St John**. The church, run by nuns, is not always open to the public but from nearby there is a marvellous view of the surrounding countryside. Also worth visiting, near the centre of the village, is the **Convent of Our Sisters of Zion**, a delightful Provence-style pension taking in a small number of guests with well-tended orchards and groves.

The next destination is the **Hadassah Ein Kerem Hospital**, visited for the famous ★ **Chagall Windows** (Sunday to Thursday 8am–3.45pm, Friday 8am–12.45pm, closed Saturday) located in the synagogue near the main entrance and executed by the Jewish artist Marc Chagall in 1961. It is only several kilometres west of the village but the hilly terrain makes the driving distance considerably longer. From Ein Kerem, continue along highway 386 before taking the clearly marked side road on the left. Each of the 12 windows represents one of the ancient tribes of Israel, portraying them in rich and vivid colours with abstract designs. Two of the windows were replaced after shelling during the Six Day War, while several others still have bullet holes.

Church of the Visitation mosaic

The drive westwards through the **Sorek Valley** along highway 386 is considered the most beautiful landscape on the Mediterranean side of Jerusalem. The steep rugged hillsides, the pine forests and the small stream snaking alongside the road are spoiled only by the smell of sewage which occasionally pollutes the water. The Jerusalem–Tel Aviv railway line also winds through this part of the mountainside and it is worth taking the train for this scenic section of the track.

At the Bar Giora Junction road number 3866 runs northwest on the ridge of the hill top and through the **American Independence Park**. There are attractive picnic areas and children's playgrounds along here. In the middle of the park, a road to the right leads down to the ★ **Sorek Cave** (Sunday to Thursday 8am–4pm, Friday 8am–2pm, closed Saturday). Some 25 million years old, this cave was discovered by chance during quarrying in 1968. The impressive stalagtite and stalagmite formations are attractively highlighted by colourful lighting and strategically placed walkways. Photography is allowed on Friday mornings only.

Beit Guvrin caves

Fans of caves will also enjoy **Beit Guvrin**, which can be reached along highway 38 some 20km (13 miles) south of Beit Shemesh. This road passes through the pastoral **Valley of Ela** where the legendary battle between David and Goliath is believed to have taken place. Beit Guvrin was an important town in Roman times and near the Nekhusha junction are some Crusader ruins. But of most interest are the various caves reached along the small road running south opposite the archaeological site. These include the Bell Caves, some impressive, large white domed caves which were quarried by the Romans, some underground burial chambers and dug-out caves that were used as hideouts during the Jewish revolt against the Romans.

Valley of Ela

Excursion 2

Bethlehem

**Rachel's Tomb – Church of the Nativity – Beit Sahur
– Hebron** *See map on page 48*

Located just 10km (6 miles) south of Jerusalem, Bethlehem is one of the most sacred places in Christendom.
Revered as the birthplace of Christ, the town has many
Old Testament associations. Rachel, the second wife of
Jacob, is buried near the northern entrance to the town,
while Ruth the Moabite was courted by Boaz in fields
nearby, and last but by no means least King David was
born here. Nevertheless, the city is not considered to have
any sacred status by Jews.

Bethlehem has been part of the Palestinian Autonomous
region since 1995, and while there are no concerns about
safety here, before visiting other attractions in the region
such as Hebron it is worth taking advice on the prevail-
ing security situation.

Follow the star

51

Derekh Khevron leads south through the suburbs of
Jerusalem. The kibbutz of Ramat Rachel marked the border between Israel and Jordan before 1967, while today
the new neighbourhood of Gilo overlooks Bethlehem, virtually linking Jerusalem and the Palestinian town. To the
east of the highway is a splendid view of the Judean Desert.

Less than a kilometre past the entrance to Gilo is the
checkpoint between Israel and the Palestinian autonomous
zone. Several hundred metres further south on the right
is **Rachel's Tomb**, believed to be the burial site of Jacob's
second wife and the mother of Benjamin. The white-
domed shrine was erected in the mid-19th century by the
Anglo-Jewish philanthropist Moses Montefiore. The tomb
attracts Jewish women who pray for fertility or a safe birth.

Immediately after the tomb there is a fork in the highway and the road to the left, Manger Street, leads into
the heart of **Bethlehem**. Bethlehem is a very graceful, hilltop town with a tranquil, relaxing atmosphere. The residents are friendly and welcoming of tourists, not least
because this is how they make their livelihood. But beneath the picturesque exterior, Bethlehem, though officially at peace and firmly in the hands of the Palestinians,
has social tensions. About half of the town's 50,000 residents are Christian and half Muslim and the Christians
fear their traditional hegemony over Bethlehem is being
threatened. Moreover, the Christians themselves have historically fought bitterly over the ★★★ **Church of Nativity** which is owned jointly by the Roman Catholic, Greek
Orthodox and Armenian Orthodox churches.

Bethlehem: a Christian and Muslim mix

Church of the Nativity

Located in Manger Square, the Church of Nativity is one of Christianity's oldest, continually functioning churches. Originally built in the 4th century by Constantine the Great, the church was added to by Justinian the Great in the 6th century. From 1099 onwards the Crusaders elevated the church to cathedral status and used it for the coronations of their kings. After the defeat of the Crusaders the church underwent centuries of neglect, not due to any fault of the town's Muslim masters but because the three churches who own various parts of the church always squabbled over who had the privilege of undertaking repairs. The inter-church hostility reached its climax in the 19th century when a star placed by the Greek Orthodox in a part of the church claimed by the Catholics resulted in the Crimean War. The Ottoman Turks removed the star and the Russian Orthodox, backing their Greek brethren, issued an ultimatum to the Turks to replace the star. The Turks refused and Russia went to war against Turkey who were backed by the British and French.

The most sacred part of the nativity complex is the **Cave of the Nativity** beneath the front of the church. A star marks the very site where it is believed that Christ was born and bears the Latin inscription, 'Here Jesus Christ was born of the Virgin Mary'. Adjacent to the church is **St Catherine's Church**, a modern Catholic establishment from where midnight mass is broadcast around the world each year.

St Catherine's Church

Though the three owners of the church agree that this was the exact site where Christ was born, each celebrates Christmas on a different date. The Catholics on 25 December, the Greek Orthodox according to 25 December on the Julian calendar (6 January on our Gregorian calendar) and the Armenians on 14 January.

Other sites of interest in Bethlehem include the **Milk Grotto Church**, just down Milk Grotto street running eastwards from Manger Square. Legend has it that the floor is white because some of Mary's milk splashed to the floor while she was feeding the infant Jesus. Not surprisingly, Christian women having difficulties breastfeeding their babies visit the church to help their lactation. In addition, Manger Square is a pleasant place to browse through souvenir shops and lounge around enjoying a meal in one of the restaurants.

The Milk Grotto Church

On the eastern fringes of Bethlehem is the village of **Beit Sahur** (Arabic for 'House of the Shepherd'). It is claimed that in one of the fields by the village, called **The Shepherd's Field**, the angel appeared before the shepherds 'watching their flocks by night' and announced the birth of Christ. Another field on the west of the village is supposedly where Boaz courted Ruth.

There are many important sites worth visiting to the south and east of Bethlehem but before doing so it is worth checking on the security situation.

Situated on highway 356 south of Beit Sahur, **Herodion** was a lavish desert fortress and palace built by Herod. This is an impressive site distinguishable from afar because it looks like the mouth of a volcano; it also offers a commanding view of the surrounding desert.

Cistern at Herodion

To the east of Beit Sahur, perched on the edge of a cliff overlooking the Kidron stream in splendid isolation amid the Judean Desert, a breathtaking sweep of billowing, barren rocks leading down to the Dead Sea, is the ★★ **Mar Saba** monastery. Established by St Saba in 492, the monastery was rebuilt by its Greek Orthodox owners after an earthquake in 1834. However, before visiting Mar Saba it should be borne in mind firstly that women are not admitted to the monastery, though the stunning location still makes a visit worthwhile. Secondly, though maps make access seem straightforward, it is easy to take the wrong turn in several Arab villages en route. Only the adventurous are advised to undertake this trip without a guide or on a formal tour.

53

Likewise **Hebron**, 16km (10 miles) south of Bethlehem, is only for the brave. This ancient city has been at the very heart of the Israeli-Palestinian conflict in the 20th century and was the last major city on the West Bank to come under Palestinian rule. Even so the **Cave of Machpelah** (The Tomb of the Patriarchs) remains under Israeli control. The Cave, which is closed more than it is open, due to the security situation and various festivals, contains the tombs of Abraham and Sarah, Isaac and Rebecca and Jacob and Leah. Hebron can be reached either via Bethlehem or directly from Jerusalem via a series of new tunnels and a bridge starting in Gilo.

Mar Saba monastery

Wadi Kelt

Excursion 3

Jericho and the Dead Sea

Wadi Kelt – St George's Monastery – Jericho – Dead Sea *See map on page 48*

This excursion down to the lowest point on earth, 400 metres (1,300ft) below sea level, through inspiring desert terrain, includes Jericho, the beautiful biblical oasis which was settled over 8,000 years ago. Floating in the nearby highly salty Dead Sea is also a special experience that should not be missed.

The road down to the Dead Sea passes through the stirring rocky and rugged landscape of the Judean Desert. Just after the junction with highway 458, at the peak of a hill, is the **Inn of the Good Samaritan** where Christians believe that Christ's encounter with the good Samaritan took place. The vastness and stark tranquillity of the desert has drawn monastics and hermits for centuries and it is easy to understand the attraction.

Greek-Orthodox monk at St George's Monastery

A detour to Jericho via the old Roman road rather than along the main highway, follows ★ **Wadi Kelt**, an attractive ribbon of lush green amid the arid brown and yellow hues of the desert. This route can be reached by turning left immediately before Mitspe Yerikho and following the orange signs. About 4km (2½ miles) down the narrow desert road is a staircase leading down to ★ **St George's Monastery** (Monday to Saturday 8am–5pm) first built in the 5th century. The present edifice clinging to the side of the canyon cliff was completed by the Greek Orthodox in 1901. Surrounded by palm trees, the location is idyllically remote. The monastery includes a 6th-century

mosaic floor and an ossiary containing the skulls of dozens of martyred monks.

The road leads down to ★★ **Jericho**, a broad expanse of green in the desert which has been a Palestinian autonomous zone since 1994. Jericho is located in the Great Syrian African Rift Valley and, while the town is pleasantly warm in the winter, especially after the chilly mountain climate of Jerusalem, it is blisteringly hot in the summer. Jericho claims to be the oldest town in the world on the basis of wooden walls carbon dated as 8,000 years old. These can be found at **Tel Jericho** (daily 8am–5pm) which is near the northern entrance to the town. Nearby is **Hisham's Palace**, an 8th-century winter palace with exceptionally well preserved mosaics. Another Jericho attraction is the **Monastery of the Temptation** (Quarantal), located half way up the mountainside behind Tel Jericho. The Greek Orthodox monastery offers a breathtaking panorama of the Jordan Valley, Jericho and the Dead Sea. According to Christian tradition, Christ was brought here by the Devil, who tempted him with control over all that he saw.

Several kilometres east of Jericho the **Allenby Bridge** leads over the River Jordan, in fact nothing more than a broad stream, into the Hashemite Kingdom of Jordan.

Several kilometres south of Jericho is the ★★ **Dead Sea**, so named because the excessive amount of salt in the water has killed off marine life. The Dead Sea is in fact a lake some 77km (49 miles) long and 10km (6 miles) across at its widest point. Visitors love to be photographed floating in the sea and the nearest place to be able to enter the water (with showers nearby) is at the **Kalya** water park. The showers are mandatory because the water is slimy and smelly and the salt will cause agonising stinging over any wounds. Menstruating women should not enter the water.

It is worth travelling further south to the **Ein Fashkha** nature reserve (daily 8am–5pm; closes 4pm in the winter) to take a dip. These freshwater pools are a favourite spot for ornithologists especially in the spring and autumn when birds migrating between Europe and Africa stop off making their way along the rift valley.

Though the water does feel very uncomfortable, the Dead Sea is actually extremely healthy. The minerals in the sea include bromine which acts as a sedative to soothe the nerves and iodine and magnesium which smooth the skin and are especially beneficial for conditions like psoriasis, rheumatism and arthritis. Treatment programmes are offered by medical professionals at **Ein Gedi** and at the hotels in **Ein Bokek** which usually involve being cov-

Biblical Jericho

Hisham's Palace

Dead Sea bathing

Medicinal mud

ered in Dead Sea mud. The medicinal properties of the region are recognised by physicians and some European national health plans offer subisidised trips to the Dead Sea. A further advantage of the area is that the evaporating gases from the sea filter out many of the sun's harmful rays reducing the risk of sunburn despite searing summer temperatures.

Israel also mines these minerals and the Dead Sea Works near the site of the infamous biblical city of Sedom at the southern end of the sea exports some $600 million worth of minerals annually.

Other sites of interest by the Dead Sea include **Kumran** (Saturday to Thursday 8am–5pm, closed Sunday) where the Dead Sea Scrolls were discovered. Visitors can usually only get a distant glimpse of the hillside cave where

Caves of Kumran

a Bedouin shepherd boy found the scrolls and must make do with a reconstructed Essene settlement. The Essenes were an ascetic Jewish sect who lived during the time of Christ. Some even practised celibacy and it is assumed that they were a deep influence on Christ. The scrolls are today housed in the Shrine of the Book (*see page 42*).

Ein Gedi, half way down the coast of the Dead Sea, has a health spa, and there are several interesting hikes here up mountain gorges including **Nakhal David**, which involves a 20 minute walk to **David's Spring** outside a cave where it is believed that David hid from Saul after the two had argued. **Nakhal Arugot**, 1km (½ mile) to the south, involves a longer climb to a refreshing desert waterfall and icy cool pools for bathing.

Situated 13km (8 miles) to south of Ein Gedi, at the southern end of the Dead Sea, more than 2 hours' drive from Jerusalem, the mighty fortress of ★★ **Masada** (daily from sunrise until 4pm) stands sentinel on an isolated, 400-metre high (1,300ft) rocky plateau. This is the remains of a Herodian fortified palace, which according to contemporary records was quite magnificent in its day. But 70 years after Herod's death, it became the setting for the final chapter of the Jewish rebellion against the Romans, which ended here in 73AD, three years after the fall of Jerusalem. The rebels, who were using the fortress as their sanctuary, had held out against Rome for seven years before 15,000 legionnaires began building a ramp to the summit. During the final onslaught, more than 1,000 Jews committed suicide rather than surrender. The defenders' heroic legacy has survived and since the founding of the modern state of Israel, Masada has been a symbol of the Israelis' determination to defend themselves.

The hilltop fortress, which is accessible by cable car, also offers a superb aerial view of the region.

Ritual bath at Masada

Excursion 4

Tel Aviv is worlds apart

Tel Aviv

Tel Aviv – Jaffa *See map on page 48*

Tel Aviv is only 59km (37 miles) from Jerusalem and yet the two cities are worlds apart. 'Jerusalem prays while Tel Aviv plays' goes the saying, but they also work hard in Tel Aviv, which is the country's commercial capital. The city has miles of golden Mediterranean beaches and is proud of its restaurants and nightlife. Describing itself as the 'city that never stops', Tel Aviv has a hedonistic and brash life style in contrast to Jerusalem's piety and reserve. The climate is also different. Tel Aviv is warmer in the winter, but in the summer high humidity compared to the dryness of the inland hills can make all of the coastal plain unbearable.

Established in 1909 just north of the biblical port of Jaffa, the city grew rapidly and soon became the leading urban centre of the newly emerging Jewish state. Today Tel Aviv is at the heart of a conurbation housing more than 2 million people. Tel Aviv is a 45-minute drive or bus ride from Jerusalem along highway 1, although dense traffic can make the journey longer.

A city on the beach

Highway 1 leads westwards from Jerusalem, twisting through the Judean Hills for 20km (13 miles) before descending to the flat plains. Greater Tel Aviv unofficially starts from Ben Gurion Airport and in the distance the high rise office buildings shimmer behind a mixture of heat haze and urban pollution. Israel believes in washing dirty linen in public and Tel Aviv welcomes visitors with a huge rubbish tip to the right of the highway past the Gannot Interchange.

Tel Aviv actually begins as highway 1 sweeps north into the Ayalon Freeway, the main artery through the city. Much of the area's commercial activity takes place around the Ayalon such as at Ramat Gan's **Diamond Exchange** complex immediately north of the Ha-Rakevet Interchange where over $4 billion worth of diamonds are polished and exported annually. **The Harry Oppenheimer Diamond Museum** (Sunday to Thursday 10am–4pm, closed Friday and Saturday) tells the story of these valuable gems.

The Diamond Exchange

The ★★**Diaspora Museum** (Sunday to Thursday 10am–5pm also Wednesday until 7pm, closed Friday and Saturday) is located in Klausner Street adjacent to Tel Aviv University. This can be reached west along Rokakh from the Rokakh Interchange, north towards Haifa along Derekh Namir and east along Levanon. Klausner is parallel to Levanon to the east.

The Museum tells the story of the Jewish people in the Diaspora and how they retained their identity for 2,000 years despite persecution and assimilation. When the Museum opened its doors in the 1970s it set an innovative trend by presenting a story through visual aids rather than exhibiting artifacts.

Excavations at the Eretz Israel Museum

The ★**Eretz Israel Museum** (Sunday to Friday 9am–1pm, Tuesday also 4–7pm and Saturday 10am–1pm) is located at the junction of Levanon and Derekh Namir. Revolving around the excavations of Tel Kasila, a settlement spanning 12 civilisations, the surrounding pavilions contain exhibitions of coins, ceramics, copper, ancient tools, glass, and the history of the alphabet.

The River Yarkon

Shderot Rokakh runs westward towards the sea and parallel to the **River Yarkon**. The Yarkon Park on the banks of the river offers a welcome escape from urban concrete and it is possible to go boating on the water. From Tel Aviv port beneath the start of Ha-Yarkon Street it is possible to walk along the Promenade all the way to Jaffa some 4 km (2½ miles) to the south. The glorious white expanse of sand is Israel's equivalent of the Corniche or Copacabana. The most popular, and on Saturday overcrowded beaches, are from the **Marina** southwards. Women often prefer the religious beach between the port and the Hilton because all men including the local gigolos are prohibited from entering on Sunday, Tuesday and Thursday. Beware the deceptively strong currents which claim nearly 100 lives annually along Israel's entire coastline.

Just inland from the beaches are Tel Aviv's hot spots. **Kikar ha-Medina** in the north contains the city's most exclusive stores, while **Dizengoff** remains a bustling thoroughfare but is passé. **Shenkin**, a narrow street running eastwards from Allenby is the fashionable place to be seen, and **Florentin**, a ramshackle neighbourhood further south near Jaffa is emerging as a trendy bohemian hang out. **Kerem ha-Teimanim** just north of Neve Tsedek has some of the city's best restaurants and it adjoins the **Carmel Market** (Ha-Carmel), the place to buy fresh food or bargains. Nearby is **Nahlat Binyamin Street**, a pleasant pedestrian precinct with streetside cafés. **Neve Tsedek** itself, between the beach and the city's financial district actually pre-dates Tel Aviv having been established in 1886 as a Jewish suburb of Jaffa. Today the quarter is being gentrified and expensive properties exist alongside slums. The centrepiece of the neighbourhood is the **Suzan Dalal Centre**, a renovated 19th-century high school which contains a theatre and is home to the Batsheva and Inbal Dance Companies.

Carmel Market

Indeed Tel Avivis are proud culture vultures and the **Mann Auditorium** along Dizengoff is where the Israel Philharmonic Orchestra is based, while the adjacent **Habima Theatre** is home of the national theatre company. This fine example of Bauhaus architecture was built in 1935 and is one of some 4,000 Bauhaus buildings which characterise Tel Aviv's contemporary countenance. The recently completed **Tel Aviv Centre for the Performing Arts** in Sha'ul ha-Melekh houses the New Israel Opera and next door is the **Tel Aviv Museum of Art** (Sunday to Thursday 10am–9.30pm, Friday 10am–2pm, Saturday 7–10pm) exhibiting the most comprehensive collection of art in Israel.

59

Young art connoisseurs

★★ **Jaffa**, officially part of Tel Aviv since 1950, retains its own distinct character. Established 4,000 years ago it was from here that wood was imported to build Solomon's Temple and Jonah set sail on his ill-fated voyage. Legend has it that Andromeda was exposed to the sea monster from the rock off the coast. Old Jaffa was renovated in 1963 into an attractive network of alleyways with art galleries and other exclusive stores. The Old Port with its fishing smacks and expensive yachts has some good quality fish restaurants and also worth visiting is the Flea Market which has a diverse selection of antiques.

A Jaffa minaret

Despite its biblical connections the city has little Judaic significance but Christians will be interested in **Simon the Tanner's House** (daily 8am–7pm) where Peter is said to have received divine instruction to preach to non-Jews. Some of Jaffa's most conspicuous buildings are churches, including **St Peter's**, a Franciscan monastery. It was built in the 17th century on the foundations of the former fortress of Jaffa, remains of which can be seen in the monastery cellar.

The monastery itself provides a fine view of the legendary Andromeda Rock.

Architecture and Art

With religion playing the central role in the historical development of the Holy City, it is no surprise that the city has a rich heritage of synagogues, mosques and churches. But visitors expecting inspiring works of religious art in Jerusalem are likely to be disappointed. Both orthodox Jews and Muslims follow the biblical prohibition of 'graven images' making only abstract art acceptable. And though the concept of Jerusalem was always central to Christianity, European leaders sent small change for the construction of churches, keeping the major funds for cathedrals at home in Rome and Constantinople, London and Paris.

Sadly, the Romans did an effective job of razing the city to the ground in AD136 so besides an abundance of archaeological remains, no Jewish architectural riches remain from the biblical period. The Byzantines built modest chapels on the sacred sites but most were destroyed by Persians in the 7th century or by the 11th-century Muslim Caliph Al-Hakim. The Crusaders built the existing Church of the Holy Sepulchre which is an unexceptional hotch potch of icons and frescoes.

Under ground in the City of David

In fact, Jerusalem possesses few ancient buildings which are truly works of art. The one glorious exception is the Dome of the Rock, the world's oldest Muslim monument, built on the Temple Mount in 691 by Caliph Abd El Malik. The striking exterior – actually 16th-century – with its tile ornamentation, geometrical and floral themes and exquisite calligraphy shows how Islam has developed abstract art forms in accordance with the need to avoid graven images. In contrast, the El Aqsa Mosque is a far more austere building, though the dozens of Persian rugs which carpet the floor lend a sense of lavishness.

El Aqsa Mosque

The Mamelukes introduced a distinctive use of coloured stones, as seen in buildings in the Mameluke Quarter, the part of the Muslim quarter closest to the Western Wall. The Ottomans, too, neglected the city, with the exception of Suleiman the Magnificent who built the Old City Walls and some attractive late 19th-century residential houses. The 19th-century German architect Conrad Schick adapted the Turkish style to build some attractive homes around Hanevi'im Street and he also designed Me'a She'arim. One such large Ottoman style house was occupied by Anna Ticho, the city's foremost landscape artist.

But while it is over 3,000 years since King David made Jerusalem his capital, not much remains from before the mid-19th century when the great European powers began building religious institutions in Jerusalem as a form of imperialist expression, while the advent of Zionism saw the Jews embark on major projects too.

61

Despite the fact that each nation built in its own national style, the use of Jerusalem stone on the facades renders a distinct harmony. Amazingly, the Italian Hospital, built in medieval Florentine style, does not seem to clash with the Muscovite Holy Trinity Cathedral or the tall German bell tower of the Church of the Redeemer. The British mandatory authority passed a by-law requiring all buildings to be faced with Jerusalem stone and the Israelis extended the edict, save for a period after 1948 when the need for cheap building seemed more urgent than aesthetics.

Modern Israeli architecture has been aimed at consolidating the city's position as the country's capital. The Knesset, Israel's parliament, is built in neo-classical style, much to the chagrin of Jewish purists. Inside are three tapestries and a mosaic by the Russian born Jewish artist Marc Chagall depicting Jewish history. Chagall's most famous work locally is the stained glass windows of the 12 tribes at Hadassah Hospital (see *Excursion 1, page 49*).

62

The Supreme Court

Elsewhere the Supreme Court, looking unexceptionally solid from the outside, has a complex interior which uses light and geometric shapes in a thought provoking way. The Israel Museum is designed like an Arab village with a series of pavilions on the hillside, while the Hebrew University on Mount Scopus is meant to mirror the Old City walls but looks more like a fortress. The modern Mormon University nearby blends delightfully into the hillside and is one of the city's more successful modern structures.

The newly built Jewish Quarter in the Old City has effectively recreated the modest narrow alleyways of the destroyed neighbourhood, but the Great Synagogue has been criticised by many Jews because of its cathedral-like rather than traditional synagogue proportions. Occasional ugly errors aside, Jerusalem's stone faced buildings, in hues of pink, beige and cream, are an integral part of the charm of this most enchanting of cities.

Israel Museum: Hadrian's bust and the Shrine of the Book

The Performing Arts

Jerusalem has no major theatre or dance companies based in the city, leaving the Jerusalem Symphony Orchestra (JSO) as the Holy City's only major cultural ambassador. However, Jerusalem is blessed with excellent theatres and concert halls which regularly draw the best performing artists from elsewhere in Israel and around the world.

Established in 1938, world-class musicians Daniel Barenboim, Yitzhak Perlman and Pinchas Zuckerman all had their first major performing opportunities with the JSO. Specialising in the works of Mahler and Mendelsohn, violinist Isaac Stern makes frequent guest appearances with the orchestra.

The JSO is based at the Henry Crown Symphony Hall, part of the Jerusalem Centre for the Performing Arts encompassing the Jerusalem Theatre and several smaller theatres. The Jerusalem Theatre frequently stages performances of Israel's two best-known theatre companies – the Habimah and the Carmeri (both Tel Aviv based) and though the plays are in Hebrew, simultaneous translations are provided in English. In addition, the JEST amateur theatre company, made up of English-speaking immigrants, offers creditable productions. Israel's well known dance troupes – the Batsheva, Bat Dor, Inbal and Kibbutz Dance Companies all perform in Jerusalem.

Israel Festival at Sultan's Pool

The best time to be in Jerusalem from the performing arts point of view is during the annual Israel Festival in late May and early June. This month-long feast of the best theatre and dance from around the world is headquartered at the Jerusalem Centre for the Performing Arts but also includes performances at a range of other unique venues. These include the Sultan's Pool, which must be one of the world's most delightful amphitheatres, located in a romantic setting beneath the Old City walls in the Hinnom Valley. Nearby is the Khan Theatre, formerly a warehouse for the railway station opposite but delightfully restored and converted into a small theatre. Other venues include the Jerusalem International Congress Centre, which has the city's largest concert hall, the Hebrew University Amphitheatre, possessing a marvellous view over the Judean Desert, and the Gerard Behard Theatre.

'King David' plays at the Zion Gate

Another important annual cultural event is the Liturgica concerts of religious classical music which take place over the Christmas period and include orchestras and choirs from around the world singing and playing Jewish, Christian and Muslim music.

Top international and local pop stars frequently perform in Jerusalem. For details about the performing arts read the *Jerusalem Post*, or contact tickets agencies Bimot, 8 Shamai, tel: 6240896; Klaim, 12 Shamai, tel: 6256869.

Street theatre

Religious and Other Festivals

The Jewish year follows a lunar-solar calendar with twelve lunar months per year plus a leap month every two to three years to bring the calendar in line with the solar year. This means Jewish festivals can vary by up to a month in the Gregorian calendar. Religious festivals aside, Israelis use the Gregorian calendar. Jewish festivals, like the sabbath, last from sunset to sunset.

The Muslim calendar is completely lunar with 12 months per year. Festivals rotate backwards through the Gregorian calendar and it is therefore impossible to anchor particular Muslim festivals to corresponding Gregorian months. The principal festivals are: New Year; Mohammed's Birthday; Ramadan (a one-month fast during daylight hours with feasts after sunset); Id El Fitr (Conclusion of Ramadan); and Id El Adha (Feast of the Sacrifice).

January/February

Orthodox Christmas: The local Christian community is mainly Orthodox and thus celebrates Christmas according to the Julian calendar on 6 January.

Tu B'Shvat: the Jewish New Year for trees is celebrated in late January or early February with tree planting ceremonies around the country.

March/April

Purim reveller

Purim, which falls during March, has a carnival atmosphere. The festival commemorates the deliverance of the Jews from destruction in Persia and it is traditional for Jews to party in fancy dress and get drunk so as not to be able to tell good from evil. Jerusalem usually arranges municipal entertainment in the Ben Yehuda Street Mall.

Pesach (Passover), which is celebrated in late March or April, recalls the exodus of the Jews from Egypt. During the week-long festival bread and yeast products are not eaten (except in the Arab sector). The first and last days of Pesach are public holidays.

Easter falls on the weekend after the first day of Pesach. The highlight is the Good Friday procession along the Via Dolorosa in Jerusalem.

Passover meal

Holocaust Day in April (sometimes early May) commemorates the six million Jews who were killed by the Nazis. All places of entertainment are closed.

Independence Day

May/June

Memorial Day in early May (sometimes late April) commemorates members of Israeli forces who have died in defence of the country. All places of entertainment are closed.

Independence Day in early May (sometimes late April) is a public holiday celebrating Israel's independence in

Easter parade

1948. On the eve of the festival the city streets are jam packed with merrymakers hitting plastic hammers (of freedom) on the heads of passers-by.

Lag B'Omer in May is an Israeli bonfire night and celebrates a range of historical miracles.

Shavuot (Pentecost) in late May or early June commemorates the giving of the Torah to the Jews on Mount Sinai. It is also a harvest festival and public holiday.

July/August
Tisha B'Av in late July/early August is a fast day commemorating the destruction of the Temple.

Tu B'Av in August marks the beginning of the grape harvest and is the festival for young lovers, who tradition dictates should get drunk on wine and romance.

September/October
Rosh Ha'Shana, the Jewish New Year in early to mid September is a two day public holiday. Jews traditionally eat apples and honey for a sweet year.

Yom Kippur, the holiest day in the Jewish calendar is a 25-hour fast asking for forgiveness from God. Everything is closed and no traffic is allowed on the roads.

Succot (Tabernacles), commemorates the 40 years the Jews spent wandering in the desert. Families build small tabernacles and eat their meals inside. The first and last days of this eight day festival are public holidays.

November/December
Chanukah is an eight-day festival of lights in which candles are lit each night to commemorate the re-dedication of the Temple after the victory over the Greeks. Gifts are given to children.

Christmas: This is where it all originally happened. The highlight is Midnight Mass in Bethlehem's Manger Square.

Chanukah at the Western Wall

65

Food and Drink

Opposite: fresh off the press

Jerusalem cuisine reflects the cosmopolitan composition of the city and also the characteristic preferences of the west. Middle Eastern cooking dominates both the Jewish and Arab sectors of the city but there are plenty of Chinese, Italian, French and Indian restaurants to choose from, not to mention McDonald's, Kentucky Fried Chicken etc.

However, most recommended is local Middle Eastern food, especially the hors d'oeuvres salads such as *humus* (chick peas), *tehina* (sesame seeds), *taboule* etc., which eaten with pita bread make a filling, healthy and inexpensive meal. Fish and meat are often disappointing. Local fish, though well seasoned, is leaner than varieties caught off Europe and America, and meat, which according to kosher laws must have all blood drained out, is often desiccated though imaginatively prepared.

A plate of chick peas and piles of olives

Kosher law requirements also mean that meat and dairy products cannot be served together so there is no butter on bread when eating meat, or milk in coffee afterwards. This separation is great for vegetarians who can be assured of meat-free meals in dairy restaurants. Visitors may be disappointed to discover that traditional Ashkenazi Eastern European cooking is very difficult to find.

Israelis enjoy their food and restaurants will serve large, well spiced portions. Hotels often lean too far to accommodate English speaking guests and make the food too bland. Generally, hotels will serve a very large buffet breakfast with lots of fruit, vegetables, fish, cheeses and cereals, so lunch need only be a snack.

The service, even in expensive Israeli restaurants, tends to be informal and sloppy. In part because of this poor service, expensive Israeli restaurants can be disappointing when compared to their European counterparts. On the other hand, the average standard of cuisine in Israel is high and just picking out an ordinary looking restaurant is likely to be a pleasant surprise. Cheap and healthy are the falafel bars, concentrated in Makhane Yehuda market and along Hamelekh George, that for about $2 offer these fried chick pea balls in pita bread with chips and as much salad as you can eat.

Israelis drink alcohol in very modest proportions and suspiciously view anybody, who drinks say three pints of beer daily, as a hardened alcoholic. There are some good local wines but these tend to be expensive, while there are few varieties of beer, most of it lager, and much of it flat. Despite this there are large numbers of pubs and bars which are mainly night spots, and are therefore listed in the nightlife section. Most Israelis will nurse several drinks all night and usually go to pubs for a meal, convivial atmosphere and music.

Fresh bagels

67

Al fresco dining

The place to go for hamburgers

Coffee break

Restaurant selection

Prices per person in the following restaurant guide: $ = up to $20 $$ = up to $40, $$$ = more than $40.

Mishkenot Sha'ananim, Yemin Moshe (behind the windmill), tel: 6254424. High-quality French cuisine (not kosher) with an inspirational view of the Old City walls enabling diners to indulge their appetite while uplifting their souls. Try the fillet steak. $$$

Cow on the Roof, Jerusalem Sheraton Plaza Hotel, King George Street, tel: 6228133. One of the city's best known exclusive restaurants offers excellent beef dishes as the name implies but is not on the roof but rather in the hotel's basement. Kosher. $$$

Chez Simon, 15 Shamai Street, tel: 6255602. Long established restaurant with excellent local cuisine. $$$

Tandoori, Holiday Inn Crowne Plaza, Givat Ram., tel: 02-6588867. One of a chain of kosher Indian restaurants with an excellent selection of vegetarian dishes. $$

Philadelphia, 9 Alzaharra Street, East Jerusalem, tel: 02-6289770. The city's best known Arab-owned restaurant (not kosher). Best of all are the wide selection of savoury salads as hors d'oeuvre. $$

De La Thien, 34 Derekh Bet Lekhem, tel: 02-6732432. Stylish building and location in the German Colony with all the Chinese favourites (not kosher) $$

The Yemenite Step, 10 Yoel Salomon Street, tel: 02-6240477. Selection of traditional Yemenite foods. Try the malahwah pancakes. $

Norman's Bar & Grill, 27 Emek Refaim Street, German Colony, tel: 02-5666603. For lovers of thick, juicy American-style hamburger steaks. Kosher so don't expect cheeseburgers. Pleasantly located with a large garden in the trendy German colony. $

Eucalyptus, 7 Horkenos Street, tel: 02-6244331. Billed as a restaurant offering the ancient recipes of the Land of Israel, the owner/chef clearly has a way with herbs and spices. Try the sorrel soup and generally trust his recommendations. Kosher. $

The Citadel, 14 Hativat Yerushalayim Street, tel: 628 8887. Excellent Lebanese Arab cuisine. Romantic location near the Jaffa Gate overlooking the Sultan's Pool. $

El Gaucho, 22 Rivlin Street, Nahlat Shiva, tel: 6242227. Located in the twee streets of Nahlat Shiva, this kosher Argentinian restaurant offers good value giant-size steaks and other Latin American meat specialities. $

Mamma Mia, 38 King George Street, tel: 6248080. In the heart of town in a beautifully restored 19th-century building, this veteran Italian kosher restaurant makes its own authentic pastas, doughs and cakes combined with an imaginative array of dishes. No meat. $

Nightlife

Jerusalem has a surprisingly vibrant nightlife. In the earlier hours of the evening, young and old alike flock to the Ben Yehuda Street and Salomon Street malls, to stroll up and down, and sit down by a streetside cafe or restaurant. The busiest nights out are Thursday and Saturday and these should be avoided by those who dislike noisy crowds. Though there are plenty of pubs and discos most of these establishments tend to be frequented by a very young crowd. For the most part, older Israelis will find a restaurant or cafe and dwell over wine or coffee for a long time after the meal.

Nightlife in pubs and discos does not get going in earnest until after 11pm. and places remain crowded until well into the small hours of the morning. The Russian Compound is the capital's busiest drinking district with activity focused on Helena HaMalkah and Monbaz, though there are also bars scattered throughout the centre of town. The Cinematheque café on Derekh Hevron is where an intellectual crowd hangs out and the cafés and restaurants of the German Colony are also busy well into the morning. The Talpiot Industrial Zone is the disco district of the city and here the action does not hot up until after midnight.

Some recommendations

Pubs:

Fink's, cnr Hahistadrut and King George Street, tel: 6234523. Has been around since the 1930s and is popular with the foreign press corps.

Glasnost, 15 Helena Hamalkah Street, tel: 6256954:. In the heart of the Russian Compound, this attracts a higher percentage of people who are not teenagers.

The Tavern, 16 Rivlin Street, tel: 6244541. Also an old established Jerusalem bar.

Hakomah Harishonah, 8 Hataasiah, Talpiot, tel: 673 6155. A new bar near the disco district in the Talpiot industrial zone.

Casso, 13 Monbaz, tel: 6257078. Round the corner from Glasnost in the Russian Compound, this bar also attracts an older clentele.

Terminal, 11 Betzalel, tel: 6231761. Near the Betzalel Art College in the centre of town, this bar attracts a trendy, intellectual crowd.

The night is still young

Discos:

Canaan, 8 HaTa'asiah Street, Talpiot, tel: 6735633: In the heart of the city's disco district.

Pack-Man, Clal Building, 97 Yafo Street, tel: 6240626. Near the centre of town.

Picture browsing

Souvenir plates and the Old City market

Shopping

When it comes to shopping Jerusalem is where East meets West. It is possible to browse through department stores in the air-conditioned comfort of shopping malls, or haggle in traditional markets. Beyond the ethnic experience of oriental markets, and the need to buy souvenirs and presents, or items of religious sentiment, there is little reason to shop in Israel. The cost of living is high. Consumer goods are 10–50 percent more expensive than Western Europe and more than double North Amercian prices.

Stores usually open 9am–7pm Sundays to Thursdays and 9am–1pm on Fridays. Shops are closed Saturdays but often open after dark until midnight. Some suburban stores may take a siesta from 2pm–4pm and Arab markets are open all day Friday and Saturday.

Souks and malls

The 'souk' is at the heart of Arab culture and strolling around the market in the Old City's Muslim Quarter is a must, not necessarily for shopping, but to taste the Orient. Enter the market either by the Jaffa Gate or the Damascus Gate and enjoy the chaotic hubbub, the smell of the spices and the good natured banter of the shopkeepers. This is not the place to buy for those embarrassed by haggling. The same items are available in West Jerusalem at fixed prices. Nevertheless, it is worth coming to the Arab market to sit in a café, sip coffee, eat *bakhlawe* and perhaps smoke a *narghile*.

The best way to buy in the souk is to price objects in the stores of West Jerusalem beforehand. This will indicate what should be paid and facilitate self-confident haggling. Items of interest in the 'souk' include olive wood carvings, *kaffiyehs* (Arab headscarfs), Hebron glassware, copper and brassware including coffee trays, ceramics (especially attractive are Armenian tiles), basketware and T-Shirts, with a range of Hebrew, Arabic and English slogans.

Brassware and other items

The Makhane Yehuda market in Jerusalem is a must for food connoisseurs. There is a wide choice of fruits and vegetables according to the season as well as pickles, dried fruits, meat and fish.

There is nothing very Middle Eastern about the Malkah Mall. But when it is not too crowded this is a comfortable and convenient places to buy gifts, especially if you are with children. The mall also has a range of fast food outlets and a multiplex cinema.

Antiquities

If you want to go home with a piece of the region's archaeological heritage, then Israel is the only country in the Middle East in which it is legal to buy antiquities providing the vendor can supply a certificate from the government's Department of Antiquities. Stores in Jerusalem's House of Quality (Derekh Hebron near the Cinematheque) such as Guy Gallery (tel: 02-6725111), or in Khutzot Hayotzer opposite the Jaffa Gate specialise in such items as shekel coins from biblical times, or ancient oil lamps, which can be purchased for very modest sums.

For Judaica try Sam Philipe, 18 King David Street, tel: 02-6259928.

Jewellery

A lot of reasonably priced handmade jewellery is available and on sale in the Ben Yehuda Street Mall, outside Bet Agron at the end of Salomon Street.

Books

Newspapers, books and maps including journals from Europe and North America can be acquired from countless stores. The best selection of English-language newspapers and books is offered by Steimatsky, 39 Jaffa Street, tel: 6250155.

Shopping for gifts

Duty Free and VAT

The duty-free shop at Ben Gurion Airport sells many of the world's best known brands of spirits and cigarettes as cheaper prices than at European airports. Shops displaying a sign 'Recommended by the Ministry of Tourism' will offer a 5 percent discount on purchases over $50.

VAT of 17 percent is refundable if the invoice is over $50 and is sealed inside a transparent bag with the goods, so that the goods and the invoice can be seen when presented to the bank in the departure hall at the airport. Refunds are in dollars. This does not apply to tobacco, electrical products and photographic equipment.

Getting There

By air

Virtually all international flights land at Ben Gurion International Airport which is 40km (25 miles) west of Jerusalem. El Al, Israel's national airline, all the major national airlines of Western Europe and Air Canada, TWA and Delta have regular flights to Israel. There are direct flights to Israel from 12 North American cities and El Al, British Airways and several charter companies fly to Israel from Heathrow, Gatwick, Stansted and Manchester. Flying time is four to five hours from Western Europe and 10 hours from East Coast USA.

Ben Gurion Airport

There is a Tourist Information Office at Ben Gurion Airport open round the clock, tel: 03-9712541.
Flight information in English: tel: 03-9723344.

There is a frequent bus service from the airport to Jerusalem as well as taxis and a shared taxi which will take passengers directly to their hotel.

By road

The borders with Lebanon and Syria are closed but there are three border crossings with Egypt and three more with Jordan. Cars are allowed to cross but travellers should expect long delays.

Egypt

The border points at Rafiah (southern tip of the Gaza Strip), Nizzana (Negev) and Taba (south of Eilat) are open every day of the year except Yom Kippur and Id El Adha). Rafiah opens 8.30am–5pm, Nizzana opens from 8am–4pm and Taba, mainly for travelling from the Sinai into Israel, opens from 7am–9pm.

Parking at a premium

Jordan

The Arava checkpoint near Eilat (07-6336812). There is a bus service from Aqaba to Eilat.

The Jordan River Crossing near Bet Shean (06-6586448) is served by buses from Amman.

The Allenby Bridge (02-9941038) near Jericho is served by buses from Amman and a taxi service to Jerusalem.

All these crossings are open 8am–4pm Sunday to Thursday, and 8am–11am Friday.

By sea

The Stability and Sol Lines offer regular sailings from Greece and Cyprus to the port of Haifa, which is 130km (80 miles) from Jerusalem.

Getting Around

Taxis and sheruts

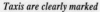

Taxis are clearly marked

Taxis are regular cars marked along the side and with a light on top. Most drivers speak some English. In town insist that the driver run the meter and for longer journeys agree a fare in advance. Ask for inter-city tariffs at your hotel. The sherut is a shared taxi that travels fixed routes between Jerusalem and other major towns. The fare is usually similar to the bus and the sherut is especially useful on the sabbath when there are no public transport services.

Buses

The bus is the essential form of public transport in Israel. The Egged national bus company runs an efficient, reasonably-priced service . There are no buses on Friday evening/Saturday except in the Arab part of the city. Students, children (5–18) and pensioners get a 5 percent discount. Children under 5 go free. Weekly and monthly tickets are good value. The Central Bus Station is on Yafo Street near the western entrance to the city, while the Arab Bus Station is opposite the Damascus Gate.

Egged information: tel: 5304555 (Jerusalem)

Trains

The railway line from Jerusalem to Tel Aviv is for scenic purposes only. There is only one train a day and it takes several hours to reach Tel Aviv compared to 45 minutes on the bus. The railway station, built by the Ottomans is in David Remez Street, tel: 6733764.

Car hire

All major companies have offices

Car hire is cheaper if booked before embarking on your vacation. The biggest local company is Eldan, and Hertz, Avis, Eurocar and others all have offices at Ben Gurion Airport as well as in Jerusalem. King David Street is where most companies have their Jerusalem offices.

Avis, 22 David Ha-Melekh tel: 6249001. **Eldan**, 24 David Ha-Melekh tel: 6252151-3. **Hertz**, 18 David Ha-Melekh tel: 6231351. **Best**, 178 Yafo tel: toll free 177-022-0015.

Air

Jerusalem Airport is at Atarot, north of the city. There are regular internal flights to Eilat, the Dead Sea, the Galilee, Haifa and elsewhere, tel: 5850980.

Kanfei Jerusalem specialises in air tours of Jerusalem, tel: 5831444.

Hitchhiking

Plotting the route

This is a national institution and there are hitchhiking stations at all major junctions.

'4

Facts for the Visitor

Visas and Passports

Citizens of Western Europe, the US, Canada and Australasia need only a valid passport. Visitors can remain in Israel for three months only after which time an extension visa must be acquired. For extensions apply to:

Ministry of Interior, 1 Shlomzion Hamalkah Street, tel: 629 0222.

Customs

European Union-style red and green channels operate in Israel. Duty-free allowances per adult include 250 cigarettes or 250 grams of tobacco, 1 litre of spirits, 2 litres of wine, 0.25 litres of perfume and gifts not exceeding $200. Expensive items such as cameras, jewellery and electronic equipment may be brought in providing they are taken out again.

Tourist Information Offices

The Israel Government Tourist Office can be contacted at the following addresses:

In the US: 350 Fifth Avenue, 19th. Floor, NY, NY. tel: 212-560 0650.
In Canada: Suite 700, 180 Bloor Street West, Toronto, Ontario tel: 416-964 3784.
In the UK: UK House, 180 Oxford Street (entrance Great Titchfield Street), London W1N 9DJ. tel: 0171-2991111.
In Jerusalem: tourist information offices at 17 Jaffa Street, tel: 02-625 8844; Jaffa Gate, tel: 628 0382

75

Currency and exchange

The New Israel Shekel is divided into 100 agorot. Notes are issued in 20NIS (grey); 50NIS (purple); 100NIS (light grey) and 200NIS (reddish-brown). Change comes in 5 agorot, 10 agorot and 50 agorot (brass), 1 shekel, 5 shekels and 10 shekels (silver). All banks offer similar exchange rates as do bureaux de change and moneychangers. Unlimited amounts of foreign currency can be bought into Israel but only $500 of shekels can be converted back to foreign currency and only $100 at the airport.

Shekels and agorots
Cash readily available

All major credit cards are accepted. If lost, phone American Express, tel: 03-5242211; Visa & Diners Club, tel: 03-5723572; Eurocard/Mastercard, tel: 03-5764444. Travellers cheques are accepted by all banks; cash machines take international credit cards.

Tipping

Hotel staff expect tips though restaurants usually add 10 percent service charge. Israelis do not tip taxis, but drivers often expect gratuities from tourists.

Taxes

17 percent VAT is charged in Israel but is exempt if hotel and car rental bills are paid in foreign currency.

Electricity

220volts AC.

Time

Israel is 2 hours ahead of GMT and 7 hours ahead of US Eastern Time. Between March and September the clock is moved one hour forward.

Hours and Holidays

Businesses operate Sunday to Thursday 8am–4pm. Stores stay open until 7pm and even later and open Friday morning and Saturday night. Banks open Sunday to Thursday 8.30am–12.30pm and Friday 8.30am–noon as well as Sunday, Tuesday and Thursday 4–5.30pm.

Everything closes down for the Sabbath from Friday afternoon until after sunset Saturday but Arab East Jerusalem stores are open on Saturday. Public holidays when Jewish West Jerusalem closes down are: Rosh Hashanah (Jewish New Year/Sept); Yom Kippur (Day of Atonement Sept/Oct); Succot (Tabernacles: Sept/Oct); Pesach (Passover March/April); Yom Ha'Atzmaut (Independence Day April/May); Shavuot (Pentecost May/June).

Communication choices

Postal and Telecommunications

Post offices display the symbol of a white stag on a red background. Jerusalem Central Post Office is at 23 Yafo (Jaffa Road), tel: 6290647 (Sunday to Thursday 8am–7pm, Friday 8am–1pm, closed Saturday). Post boxes are yellow for in-town mail and red for out of town and abroad. Stores also sell stamps and phone cards.

Phones are operated by cards, coins or credit cards. Israel's international dialling code is 972 and the country is divided into the following area codes: 02-Jerusalem; 03-Tel Aviv; 04-Haifa; 06-North; 07-South; 08-South Central; 09-North Central. To ring abroad dial 00, 1 for Canada and US, 44 for the UK.

Disabled

Visitors in need of such equipment as wheelchairs, oxygen tanks etc: Yad Sarah, 43 Haneviim Street, Jerusalem, tel: 6444444 fax: 6244493. Book at least two weeks before visit

Jerusalem for Children

All that religion, history and archaeology can be heavy going for children. But do not despair, the city has plenty of attractions designed for youngsters.

The Biblical Zoo (*see Route 7*) exhibits the animals mentioned in the Bible together with the relevant quotations and has a children's playground and petting section. The Israel Museum (*see Route 6*) has an entire Youth Wing with hands-on activities for children. The nearby Science Museum (*also Route 6*) is aimed at young minds.

The Liberty Bell Park has a puppet theatre in a railway carriage as well as an excellent playground, and the Malkah Shopping Mall has a creche that will look after children. Restaurants, other than the burger and pizza chains, rarely have special children's menus but staff will bend over backwards to pander to fussy eaters.

Children are crazy about camel rides, and there's several stationed at the Mount of Olives lookout (*see Route 3*). It may be an idea for an adult to ride along with smaller children because the height and movement of the camel can be very scary. The colour and noise of the Arab 'souk' usually fascinates youngsters and model fans will enjoy the re-creation of Second Temple Jerusalem (*see Route 7*).

Media

Visitors can stay abreast of local matters with the *Jerusalem Post,* which offers listings for local cinemas, TV programmes, religious services etc. The bi-weekly *Jerusalem Report* is also worth reading. In addition to two state owned channels and one commercial station Israelis receive some 50 channels on cable TV including BBC, CNN and Sky News. Israel's Channel One has a daily English language new broadcast at 6.15pm.

Israel Radio broadcasts include English language news programmes on Reshet Aleph at 7am, 1pm. and 5pm.

Health

Tap water is drinkable in Jerusalem and mineral water is available. The biggest health problem for visitors concerns sun and heat. Symptoms of dehydration include headaches, stomach upset, fever and diarrhoea and visitors often mistake dehydration for a foreign bug. Drink half a litre an hour when it is hot. Most pharmacists speak English and the *Jerusalem Post* will list duty pharmacies open at nights and weekends.

Medical care is expensive so insurance is mandatory. Doctors charge about $40 for a consultation. Israeli hospitals accept all emergencies.

Phone 101 for ambulances.

Police

Theft is rampant in Jerusalem but violent crime is rare. The police are helpful, especially the tourist police, tel: 6273222. Traffic police tend to be lenient with tourists.

Phone 100 for police.

Local newspapers

The police is always on hand

Accommodation

The Jerusalem region has over 10,000 hotel rooms ranging from the luxurious and very expensive through to budget priced accommodation. In addition, there are numerous youth hostels and B&B style guest houses. Two uniquely Israeli types of accommodation are kibbutz guest houses and Christian hospices. But though both sound austere for ideological and religious reasons, they are in fact comfortable places to stay and every bit as expensive as good quality hotels.

The following bands relate to prices quoted for just turning up and wanting to stay overnight. Package tour prices are less than half these amounts.

$$$ = expensive (over $150); **$$** = moderate ($90-$150); **$** = inexpensive (less than $90). High season is Christmas, Easter/Passover and the Jewish New Year; visitors are advised to book well in advance.

King David Hotel

$$$

King David Hotel, 23 Ha-Melekh David (King David Street), tel: 620 8888 fax: 623 2303. The country's leading hotel, sought after for its old-world ambiance and splendid gardens overlooking the Old City. World leaders and the rich and famous stay here, and perhaps because of this service verges on the complacent.

Laromme Hotel, 3 Jabotinsky Street, tel: 675 6666, fax: 6756777. Excellent service and stylish design and location has made this hotel, built in the early 1980s, a worthy rival of the King David.

Holiday Inn Crowne Plaza, Givat Ram., tel: 658 8888, fax: 651 4555. Formerly the Hilton, this high-rise building dominates the western entrance to the city. Convenient location if attending a conference at the adjacent International Congress Centre.

Dan Pearl, Tzahal Square, tel: 622 6666, fax: 622 6649. The city's newest hotel is fabulously located opposite the Old City walls.

American Colony Hotel

Radisson Moriah, tel: 569 5695, fax: 623 2411. Tranquil atmosphere not typical of Jerusalem even though this is a very large luxury hotel.

$$

American Colony Hotel, Nablus Street, tel: 628 5171, fax: 627 9779. The city's oldest hotel is favoured by the foreign press corps because of its location between West and East Jerusalem.

Seven Arches Hotel, tel: 627 7555, fax: 627 1319. Formerly the Inter-Continental the hotel offers a stirring view from the Mount of Olives but antagonises orthodox Jews because it is built on a desecrated Jewish cemetery.

Mount Zion, Derekh Hevron, tel: 672 4222, fax: 673 1425. A hotel with a lot of character overlooking the picturesque Hinnom Valley. The 19th-century building was converted to a hotel in the 1980s from an ophthalmology hospital.
Mitzpeh Rachel, Kibbutz Ramat Rachel, tel: 670 2555, fax: 673 3155. Within Jerusalem's city limits and offering a splendid panorama of the Judean desert.
Our Sisters of Zion, Ein Kerem, tel: 641 5738. Provence-style pension in Ein Kerem with spacious gardens filled with lemon and olive trees and tended by the nuns.
Notre Dame, Hatzakhanim opp New Gate, tel: 628 1223. Luxurious Christian Hospice located in palace like 19th-century building opposite the Old City.
YMCA, Ha-Melekh David, POB 294, tel: 625 3433. Designed by the same architects as the Empire State Building, this stylish building is opposite the King David Hotel.
Neve Ilan, D.N. Hare Yehuda (near Jerusalem), tel: 534 8111 fax: 534 8197. Pleasant hillside country club atmosphere with a commanding view of the coastal plain.

Mount Zion Hotel

$
Ron Hotel, Zion Square, tel: 625 3471 fax: 625 0707. Located in the heart of West Jerusalem, this hotel has the charm of a Central European pension.
Windmill Hotel, 3 Mendele Street, tel: 566 3111 fax: 5610964. Great location near Yemin Moshe for such an economically priced hotel.
St Andrews Scots Memorial Hospice, tel: 673 2401. A small corner of the Holy Land is forever Scotland but don't expect kippers for breakfast.

Ron Hotel

79

Bed & Breakfast
Though limited, there is a B&B central office called 'Good Morning Jerusalem' at the International Congress Centre near the Central Bus Station, tel: 651 1270 which provides information about available places.

Youth Hostels
Jaffa Gate Youth Hostel, El Khattab Sqare, tel: 589 8480. Great sightsseers location inside the Old City.
King George Hostel, 15 Ha-Melekh George, tel: 622 3498. Good location in the New City.
Ein Kerem P.O.B. 17013 Jerusalem, tel: 6416282. For those who prefer the country air.

Camping
There are two campsites on the outskirts where visitors can put up a tent and enjoy full sanitary services.
Bet Zayit, tel: 534 6217. Near the Western entrance to the city. **Ramat Rachel**, tel: 670 2555. Southeast of the city overlooking the desert.

YMCA Hostel

Index